TEQUILA & SALT

I'm Every Woman

TEQUILA & SALT

I'm Every Woman

A memoir by

Cassie Date

Fresh Ink Group
Guntersville

TEQUILA & SALT: I'M EVERY WOMAN

Copyright © 2018

Fresh Ink Group
An Imprint of:
The Fresh Ink Group, LLC
Box 931
Guntersville, AL 35976
Email: info@FreshInkGroup.com
FreshInkGroup.com

Edition 1.0   2018

As proofread and edited by Rodolfo Mazzuchi MacSwain

Book design by Ann E. Stewart / FIG

Cover by Stephen Geez / FIG

Cover art by Anik / FIG

Cataloging-in-Publication Recommendations:
BIO026000   BIOGRAPHY & AUTOBIOGRAPHY / Personal Memoirs
BIO022000   BIOGRAPHY & AUTOBIOGRAPHY / Women
BIO002000   BIOGRAPHY & AUTOBIOGRAPHY / Cultural Heritage

Library of Congress Control Number: 2018934516

Hardcover ISBN-13: 978-1-936442-35-5
Softcover ISBN-13: 978-1-936442-41-6
Ebook ISBN-13: 978-1-936442-42-3

A foreword from the editor

Fate is weird. I would have never expected to end up reading, much less editing, what I had wrongly prejudged as a mere emotional escape valve. To my great surprise, I found from the very beginning that I had before me a work either to be tasted, devoured, or chewed and digested thoroughly, depending on the reader. Or perhaps all at the same time, for such feat is also a possibility here. We have a literary iceberg in our hands, and we may choose either to marvel at its tip or else dive into the deep to contemplate the vast insights below the surface. One thing is guaranteed: the story will leave no one indifferent.

Tequila & Salt is an expression of the visceral, vital, subconscious power that we call desire, of which sexuality is merely one of many manifestations. It transgresses the norm by making public the private, the intimate, and the sexual, expressing the infinite power and beauty of the subconscious. This is the journey of a brave woman we can all fully recognize, the search for acknowledgement as a human being, shared from soul to soul.

The need to be acknowledged, that our feelings be acknowledged, is as universal as the need to breathe. Even when the wise on our planet strongly advise against having expectations, this is one which just cannot be avoided. Knowing that our feelings and emotions are understood and accepted by others is indeed powerful, and necessary for bonding. And there is yet another essential aspect in this personal validation structure: we all crave to be special to someone, as this reminds us we are important, worthy of love.

How do we deal with the reality that we are not treated as special? Can we distinguish the difference between being special and being treated as special? For when we are not treated as such, we sometimes forget we always were and will always be, nonetheless, special.

1

At some point, a few of those who forget they are special choose to begin a quest for acknowledgement in order to reclaim their power and self-respect, to feel valued for what deep inside they know they are.

Cassie Date is one of these daring mortals who one day left their comfortable numbness to reclaim their present and their future. Let the reader not be fooled by her resilience and mistake it for weakness. She set her heart to a mission, and with a vengeance. She will take a beating or seem to beg for love if it becomes necessary to stand up tall again. And in the process, she will ask herself many questions, submit herself to heart-wrenching situations, feel both desired and rejected, and get to know herself deeply... only to rise from the cleansing fire with her strength regained. In the end, all she wanted was to go home, to feel that her heart was warm and protected...

Tequila & Salt proves to be a most enjoyable reading about a woman who never gave up on herself, and an open invitation to reflection and introspection, for this could be your journey too. Your journey towards emotional survival.

I cannot thank the author enough for the privilege of adding my contribution to this honest and courageous piece. And neither can I close my introduction without a word of caution ...

Be warned, fellow reader: A single phrase in this book could stir feelings of love. Why? Because you are being acknowledged.

Rodolfo Mazzuchi MacSwain
Somewhere in France, winter of 2018

Friday, January 12th 2018
THANK YOU

When I started posting online in 2016, this whole new crowd began gathering around me. From all corners of the world. Some came and went. Others came and stayed. Loads of them, actually. Faithfully reading and commenting on my ramblings regularly. Writing me private messages. Some even on a daily basis. Patiently awaiting *Tequila & Salt* to be delivered.

And to those people - too many to name here, but you all know who you are -, I would like to offer my eternal gratitude. It was Hot Date #1 who made me aware again of my everlasting femininity. But you guys, man . . . you made me learn and grow! You made me further develop into what I am today. Feelings included.

A proud woman, content and powerful. A woman who, no matter what happens, gets up with a smile every single day! It makes me very happy to be able to share all this with you, and to continue doing it for as long as I possibly can. 😺

My 3 kids . . . What would I do without them? So patient and helpful when 'Bad Mom' was again stuck to her screen writing or chatting . . . The number of times they brought me coffee and cigarettes. The teasing once I told them about the book and its contents. And how excited they are to now have a 'writer Mom' . . . And one that is happy at that! Stay the way you are, my babes! And thank you for bearing with me! Love you to bits!

Also, a huge thank-you for G-man, Stephen Geez, full of humor and patiently suffering for almost 12 months – on and off – my rambling questions, requests, and changes; and co-ordinating this whole book project, including a huge contribution for the cover design. To the late

Ann Stewart for helping out with the administration and the final book design. And to Beem Weeks for guiding me on the social media launch.

I would like to give credit to Artist (yes, with a capital A) Anik for the artwork of the Tequila & Salt cover.

Fresh Ink Group, definitely a most wonderful guide in indie publishing.

All through most of my adult life, I was lucky enough to have a friend that proved to be so much more than just a friend. My soul sister. Always inspiring, listening, and advising. And laughing. Definitely always adding fun to just anything. That one person you may call in the middle of the night if need be. She'll always be there, putting up with me and my ramblings.

Finally, my editor. Rodolfo Mazzuchi MacSwain. *What* did *I* know about editing ? Gee! He sat down with me to work – at times around the clock - to make sure that every paragraph (!) was consistent with what I have gone through. I believe I should call him psychologist instead of editor, for that is what it felt like: therapy. I am eternally grateful, for his input was exactly what I needed to reassure that this part of my life had been essential in my becoming the woman I am today, and that my book had to be published.

Facts do not cease to exist
because they are ignored ...

-Aldous Huxley

Sunday, April 23rd 2017
AFTER THE FACTS

I have read and re-read this diary so many times. And every time I finish, I just can't believe how I managed to become so insecure about myself, so loveless about who I thought was there: the Mom. I already *was* fucking awesome before meeting Hot Date #1. Always have been. I finished my studies at age 48, ran marathons, was there for my kids, exercised my creativity. And had been a business bitch before that. I was already beautiful. Why could I not see that all was good?

Many times I have been tempted to change my ramblings. The naivety at times. The stupidity at others. But I have decided against it time and again. It was my diary, my feelings at the time, and so be it! But this truly shows me as I was, and I do hope you enjoy it.

How could I have let myself be led by my Cuban lover for just over 4 months, when I should have cut myself loose after 2.5 weeks? I mean, casual is casual, right? Fuck, was I searching for a new rock? Another stability, even if only for one or two nights per week? Was I *that* deprived of physical contact? I stated all along that I was not in love. And I wasn't. Never been and never will be. Not with Hot Date #1, that is. Why did I stay in this casual dating scene if I knew from the start it was not my thing?

But I did find my secret exciting. The sex as well, of course (always remain honest!) I truly had fun for a while. And I look back with a smile and a sigh . . .

I have also come to understand that where two fight, two are at fault. No question about it.

Of course, my almost-ex has not always been courteous to me, and he still is unhappy with what he does in his life. I learned, now that I've grown so much mentally, that neither have I helped him a lot in changing his situation over the past couple of years. All I tried to do was make him happy and keep the family together. And I *did* for a while. But trying is of no use if you are not motivated on the same level. The team was gone, and in my heart I guess I had known a long long time ago that we would never ride the same wave again.

So today, I live for myself. Not for my family. Not for other people. Just for myself. Trying to be the best example that I can be for my babes and for the people I love. I have a life again. A life filled with joy and laughter; and I am absolutely passionate about my projects.

And I keep at it now. Remaining myself. Because I need it. Because I am. I want to explore this recovered independence, and be the free spirit I have become.

I am my rock !

*Don't just stand outside your story
and hustle for your worthiness.*

Walk in it, live it, own it!

-Bréne Brown & Cassie Date

Thursday, September 1st 2016
INTRODUCTION

At what point do my own needs have priority over anyone else's, *including my kids*?

This is my life I am talking about, and I have the right to be happy. No, I owe it to myself to be happy, because life is beautiful. This gift of life may have been given to me more than once. *Yes, I do believe I have lived other lives before.* But what is the use of being alive today, if you cannot enjoy today?

In my case, the first affair was not entirely driven by sexual desire. More out of emotional neglect and an extremely long-term lack of intimacy. To me, it was craving to feel desired, needed, wanted, accepted for who I had become ... alive. No prejudice. And yes, of course, sexy (*read: having sex*), as well.

I believe those are basic and very healthy needs, which my marriage did no longer provide. I will not bother you with the reasons why my relationship did no longer 'work', as everyone has different reasons and my past is not of essence to this diary. Let's leave it at that. I believe I have tried everything for the last 12 years to make things work. I guess we have both changed in our approaches to life and have different values now than we had when we started. No hard feelings. No regrets from my side.

The point is, I have tears in my eyes while writing all this, because having been so unhappy for so long, having been thrown lemons at so many times, it makes me wonder why I didn't ask for Tequila & Salt before.

So be it! Everything happens for a reason, and there is a time for everything. These are also things I strongly believe in.

In that spirit, I started an online diary. Maybe to help out someone else who needed to know she's not alone out there, or maybe to put myself in perspective. I simply don't know. I just wanted some trace of this extraordinary experience, for this feeling to go from 'feel' to 'real'. Which, by the way, is how I came up with the pseudonym Cassie Date. Facebook didn't find 'Casual Date' an acceptable name.

Further down the road, however, I started thinking, *Who can I identify with today, at age 49?*... So many great women alive, but no stories about their deepest feelings, their secrets, their fears, and their lust. A lot of fiction. And so many women my age who are unhappy and feel 'locked-up' in their lives . . .

Then one day, a friend read over my shoulder and almost peed her pants laughing. And that is how the book idea was born. Well, here you have it . . . something to think about, something that is real. Something that is happening right now. To open your eyes. Wide. After all, this parallel life I will be talking about later is out there, and not to be ignored. To enjoy it if you want it. And if you can. I couldn't.

I am not saying I am *pro*-affair. I definitely am not! I have been a monogamous woman ever since I said 'I do' *(until Hot Date #1, that is)*. But . . . if you have tried to make things work for as long as I have, and the only end is a dead end, then what have you got to lose, right?

I chose to take matters into my own hands instead of crying on a Freudian couch. I became happy with myself in the process. Very quickly so. I have also been disappointed. And felt used. At some point, I wanted to go back to my old life, as it was much safer. Because I am definitely not cut out for the casual online dating stuff. Too many feelings and not a 'straight-fuck' type of girl. I need to feel for the person. And this is dangerous. But I went on and beyond. Bit masochistic? Maybe, but I got to know myself inside and out. I know I please, I know how to let go, I know what I do not want. And I will tell you all about it while in the process.

People definitely do not change at my age. They learn from all their different experiences and become better actors for it. I am a bad actor. This is the most important thing I learned about myself. I can pretend to be a good actor, but that does not make me one. Somehow, my feelings always get in the way.

I guess a psychologist would have a field day analyzing this part of my life!

Today, I am happy with myself, my kids, and all the life projects I am working on. No potential long-term relation on sight. But I am still wondering about nights in white satin (*or rather black, as white is way too innocent for me*) . . .

I'M IN LOVE WITH LIFE. I LIVE, I FEEL, I DO!

I guess I am a lucky woman after all . . .

I am Cassie.

You can close your eyes and pretend it is not there ...
Or you can close them and 'see' your way out.

Friday, December 25th 2015 (Yay, I'm 49!)
I REALIZE . . .

And then, you come to terms with the fact that your marriage is finally over.

At exactly 49 years of age, I realize that after years of trying, struggling, wanting to believe it would all get better one day, it definitely could not become any worse.

It's time to take back the only thing which was mine to start with . . . MY LIFE.

I am proud of my story, but more so of the fact that I am the one who wrote it. And all I did was try to survive . . .

Saturday, December 26th 2015
HERE I AM

Of course, my real name is not Cassie Date, and, of course, I do not live in New Orleans as my Facebook page indicates. (I wish!)
All the rest is real, though.

After being 'locked-up' in a loveless marriage for so long, it's not easy to open up and 'really' talk with anyone—except for my soul sister, of course, but she must be so tired of hearing the same story over and over again.

You know that feeling? You wanna say something and in your head it's all worked out, and it actually sounds like the right thing to say . . . but then, when you open your mouth, it just comes out all wrong (*hahaha*). Well, that's me!

She told me once I could sometimes be a real 'ball-breaker' (*if only she knew half of it*).

And the following poem comes to mind . . .

You will always be too much of something for someone:

Too big, too loud, too soft, too edgy.

If you round out your edges, you lose your edge.

Apologise for mistakes.

Apologise for unintentionally hurting someone—profusely!

But never ever apologise for being who you are.

Well, I believe this poem (by Danielle LaPorte) was probably written for me.

Don't get me wrong, though—people find me extremely funny and do enjoy going out with me as it will always be an evening full of fun, mojitos and laughter (no Cuba Libre nor tequila though . . . these come later).

But to start your life over with new people (and don't forget the three kids you carry with you into this new life) . . . Man, do I need to loosen up a bit! I am so fucking scared and nervous about it. And at the same time, *oh,* so excited!

I am not one to sit down and feel sorry for myself. Well, sometimes I do, but only in extreme cases. I am 49 years and one day old, and I have a life to live. Whatever it may be that makes me happy, I will do my utmost to find it.

For whatever reason: HERE I AM!

To realize all of a sudden that the ocean exists,
and with it, endless possibility ...

Sunday, December 27th 2015
FEELING DETERMINED

Desperately Seeking Susan, or rather *Bridget Jones,* comes briefly to mind—but that's just plain wrong!

I am so determined to start over at last. For me. For my kids. Hell yeah, for the whole wide world!

Decisions are made, projects worked on, and I am more aware of the immense possibilities of starting a new life 😊 . . .

Realization is awareness.
Action is survival.

Friday, January 1st 2016
PARTLY SEPARATED . . .

Yep, after almost 20 years of marriage, over a decade of struggling, and more than a year without sex—I have moved into the spare room.

Somehow, the 1st of January 2016 seems to mark the moment. It feels right.

And I sleep like a baby . . .

I was let fade away into the background, disappear.

No one crawled into my space.
No one grabbed my hand.
No one pulled me out ...

Saturday, March 26th 2016
FEELING BLUE . . .

I feel so alone . . . Despite having a soul sister who listens, comments, and doesn't judge.

I worked hard on my projects the last couple of months, and everything starts taking shape. However, the space I need for my project has not materialized as of yet. Patience.

My home situation is deteriorating in 'free-fall' style.

How do you continue living with a person who is drawing back more and more, who doesn't want to share / do anything, who comes and goes without letting us know, replies with a simple yes or no? That is, if he makes the effort of answering. And clearly doesn't care about anything to do with you any longer—including his own kids, it seems. That hurts.

But to date, he still *is* my husband by law, and he *is* the father of my 3 children. (Deal with it!)

Stonecold by Demi Lovato is playing.

That sums it up . . . I just feel soooo cold!

My youngest son was extremely depressed and tried to take his life some weeks ago for reasons unknown, other than being completely unhappy. And for the time being, he doesn't open up to anyone.

Life really sucks. Nothing seems to go as planned.

Breath in . . . and out . . . It's all it takes to live.

If I wanted to be seen,
I would have to stand up to the sun.

Friday, April 1st 2016
WEEKEND WITH THE GIRLS

Thank God for friends . . .

A wonderful weekend overseas with the girls has done me the best of good.

Sightseeing, good food, drinks, dancing *(for the girls, as I only dance if there's a piano to dance on top of)*, flirting, and, above all, LAUGHING a lot and loud.

Putting things into perspective . . . Trying to get my priorities in order . . .

Bought a hot leather jacket and a silk scarf—I deserve it.

Déjà brew:
The feeling that you've had this coffee before …

-Unknown

Wednesday, April 6th 2016
LUNCH WITH A FACEBOOK FRIEND

Oh-la-la, it was so nice to finally meet her! Have you ever experienced communicating with someone on line, and knowing that this 'feels' right? That you synchronize well with the person? That you can identify?

Well, she is witty, to the point, and soooo honest. Potential soul sister material?

We started off really well: lunch was good, and we talked a lot about relationships and their complications. About doubts and being scared. About loss, and how it all came to this being alone while still in a couple and having young children to explain matters to. "Why does Dad hardly ever have dinner with us?" "Where did Dad go?" Aaargh— I didn't know, I just didn't know. I was able to explain why I moved in to the spare room, as that had been my decision. As to the rest, maybe it would have been easier had I only known . . . But, not even that he could give me.

Man, I feel 'lifted' and at the same time extremely down, hesitant, because expressing myself in front of a stranger was something unthinkable till there and then.

And a stranger she was. We had only 'met' (a lot) on Facebook and this one face-to-face meet-up, but definitely the start of a new Friendship *(yes, with a capital 'F')*.

Her advice:

1. be independent again a.s.a.p.

2. get a boyfriend

I agreed to number 1. It would make things easier on the kids, take my mind off walking on eggs at home *(when the almost-ex decides to be there, that is)*. Shelve my projects for a while and look for a job to become financially independent again. *Why can we not see the logic in front of us, when it is so clear to others?* I had toyed with the idea and discussed it with my 'local' soul sister of 20 years. However, nothing serious ever did come out of it.

Number 2… I said no to it straight away. I am definitely not going to replace one man with another. I will do it on my own terms this time, no strings attached.

She smiled and said cunningly, "Noooo, not that kind of boyfriend" (wink). "What I mean is that you have not been a woman for a long long time, and that needs to change." (We had spoken about lack of sex by then.)

Darn! That was something to think about . . .

You see, so far my life has been pretty boring.

Yes, I was the CEO of a multi-million IT company *(was I 'hot' back then?)* Yes, I took up studies at age 45 *(and* finished with a degree 3 years later). Yes, I have exciting projects in the pipeline; and yes, I have 3 adorable kids . . .

But it hasn't got anything to do with all that. In the end, today, I'm still a housewife. I'm still cleaning and cooking. And besides an evening or weekend out with the girls every now and then *(way not often enough)*, plus some small client projects on the side, it's still pretty routine, right?

Well, that's certainly going to change ! Did I decide 3 months ago that a new life was starting? This is it.

😊

*To turn disappointment into action
and thus recover your balance.*

To go to your own emotional rescue.

Thursday, April 7th 2016
THINKING ABOUT IT . . .

And yes again. My new best friend is right . . . If I were to feel good in body *and* mind *(in that order)*, then everyone at home feels better as well. Mom's happy, everyone is happy, right?

Shit! Do I want my life back? OK, then hit the gas! Half of your life is over. Although my brain stopped at 25 and refuses to grow older, it secretly knows a bucket list should be in the making.

So I checked out a few sites the same afternoon, and decided on one *(for starters)*. Extremely anonymous, very impersonal, so unlike me.

Then messages started pouring in . . . all 300 of them within 24 hours, one after the other!

Oh, my God! There is a whole parallel life being lived out there! And I didn't know about this?

From the hugely charming 'older' man who can't seem to make it happen with his wife anymore to the 19-year-old youngster *(Yes, I'm 49 and I no longer do babysitting, honey)*. From the exhibitionist who wants to 'take you' places to the one who writes you his darkest fantasies.

Man, some people are really sick . . .

I decided to delete most of them, and had some 'conversations' with those whom I thought had 'friendship or more' potential. *How little did I know . . .*

But this is definitely NOT my thing . . .

What was I expecting?! After all, it's a casual dating site *(read: sneaky sexual encounters)*, and the monogamous bitch (me) is not into that, right? *What do I want? What do I need?* I cannot just go and snatch someone else's husband ... But then again, *I* am there as well. *I* have a husband. A soon to be *ex*-husband, but still a husband.

I feel almost sad ... Once over 35, you have to meet people like this? And the youngster ... hell, boy, get a life!—go out, have fun chasing girls your age! It's a sport! (*Been there, done that. Oh, so long ago ...*)

Then again, who am I to judge? For here I am ...

You have to understand the site is completely automated; nothing personal except for the color of your hair and eyes, your body type, your heigth, your zodiac sign, year of birth. You select some predefined 'sexy' pictures that please you, you're 'boxed' with people who have chosen similar pictures, and the site will propose potential candidates.

So, the messages you receive are not actually to you but to someone the writer fantasizes you to be. Ok, now that this is out of the way, I feel better ... Men can fantasize whatever they want, they're not thinking of me when they do. It's their *'image'* of me they fantasize about.

After having refused most of them, I received a message from someone who was clearly a foreigner, as I am in this country. I liked that. And the fact that he was not laying himself bare immediately, nor asking me if I was horny. I asked him if he could dance. He could ... salsa (*mmmmm*). I asked for his picture (*Holy mmmmm*); he asked for mine. Showed him mine, and he asked me out that same evening.

Ehh, hold on ... now? As in immediately? Tonight? What's the rush?

But a second thought came straight away, 'What the heck, I'm all alone tonight, as the kids are on a trip with Dad—let's go for it!'

I'm off for a bath and to shave my bits.

Feeling excited, feeling desired—*by a stranger looking at one picture of me? Who am I kidding?*

Bold or bald?

Friday, April 8th 2016
AM I REALLY DOING THIS?

Well, yes, I am! All of my 1m72, black medium-length hair, blue eyes—and the 1966 Capricorn is thrilled with the prospect of a potential admirer.

All Bridget-like shaving while having a bath, big smirk on my face, and in the back of my mind . . . 'Wow, easy, girl . . . what if he's a creep? What if he's everything you read in all those 300 messages?' Shiiiiit . . . He wanted me to meet at his place, which of course I wouldn't—we're meeting at a bar downtown. Holy ground.

Scary business this online dating . . .

Then the phone rings. The almost-ex. "Your son (*My son? Ours, right?*) is coming home to you. He doesn't want to stay with me any longer . . ."

REALLY? Dear son, tonight of all nights, couldn't you stay just one more night?

In view of what had happened earlier this month, I found I needed to be there for him, so I got out of my bath and sent a message to Potential Hot Date #1 to cancel for tonight. Could he do (*me*) tomorrow?

Saved from doing something stupid but exciting, and definitely not in my nature—by my own son?

Will I thank him later? Or regret it because I'll never find out what it would have been like?

Wow! Towel off, babe!

Later on . . .

Nice doing, Potential Hot Date #1 . . . He writes back straight away, saying he hasn't got time tomorrow, but from Monday to Friday OK with him (*Girlfriend? Kids?*), and if I change my mind he'll be home (*haaa!*)

Decent person that I am, I feel obliged to explain, so I reply that I would have loved to go dancing with him and bring up *(not in detail, of course)* the son-dad issue, and that I would get back to him ASAP—and without complications . . .

Potential Hot Date #1 writes straight back; he understands, he has two daughters.

In short, his kids are the same age as my two youngest. He finds me funny and honest, and he is extremely curious. *Me too, honey, me too . . .*

Shedding my skin,
and my disguise ...

Monday, April 11th 2016
SHIT … SHAVING IS NEVER A GOOD IDEA

I have this (minor, Stage I) skin condition called reverse acne . . . Now don't start looking this up on the internet, 'cause what you see there is ugly. Mine is nothing like it, but it is never a good idea to shave, as it may get infected. And of course, now of all times, it does. Very Bridget-like. It so hurts like hell . . .

Hobbit-walk in the making.

O God,
make me good …

But not yet

-Evelyn Waugh

Tuesday, April 12th 2016
SHIT AGAIN . . .

Message if I am still interested. (*Am I?*)

Yeah sure, with a cyst the size of a tennis ball between my legs (honestly, that's how big it feels).

Quick visit to the skin doctor—*He's not bad, either, by the way*—a dose of antibiotics, and off to Germany to visit two universities for my projects. At least THAT was an exciting prospect.

Leave Potential Hot Date #1 till tomorrow. Will tell him I was out of town for 2 days instead of 1 day only . . .

Freakin' lump made me lie! Lump definitely has got to go!

While clouds disappear
One by one
I'm getting ready
To jump into the deep

Wednesday, April 13th 2016
YEP, HE'S DEFINITELY NICE

Told him I was out of the country for 2 days, and that this week was difficult. But maybe next week? That is, if he was still interested. Buying time for my lump to get lost . . .

Potential Hot Date #1 is again understanding, and asks me to get back to him when I want to meet-up.

Cool dude—asks me about my projects and seems really interested in what I do, and hopes all goes as I wish . . . *Seducing tactics?*

Oh, whatever, who cares! It feels good that someone is interested in me as a person for once. And of course, *carrying a secret . . .* that's nice as well.

I've been a mom for too long—I do need to go out more!

Oh, and by the way—on the suspected 'foreigner' front—his mother tongue is Spanish (*nice, Señor*). Always wanted to learn Spanish.

And he is still excited to meet me. *What a patient Potential Hot Date #1!*

Thick skin and a positive mind
are essential to survive …

Friday, April 15th 2016
LUMP LEADING ITS OWN LIFE

Back to skin doctor—cyst needs to be surgically removed.

Holy lump . . . *No es posible* . . . What about Hot Date #1? But lump has got to go—let's do it, Doctor!

Jesus, it hurts! Lump holds on for dear life! You're ready when you're ready, right? Lumps like that cannot be forced, or there will be lots of baby lumps soon after.

So, lump stays. More antibiotics, and a huge dressing with antibiotics cream . . . Yay, Hot Date # 1, here I come! *That was the lump talking, by the way.*

Now I have to make an appointment with a plastic surgeon to discuss how to deal with the problem. Nice. More cutting and pasting. As if I hadn't had enough of this already . . .

I am not in danger
I am the danger

-Walter White

Sunday, April 17th 2016
STALKER? OR DESPERATE?

Asks me how my day was on the 14th, and tells me he'd like to meet with me soon. Wishes me a wonderful weekend on the 15th. I actually needed that. The well-wishing, that is; home front improvement is no longer on my list.

What my agenda *does* need is a Hot Date. Preferably right now. And this one doesn't seem bad at all.

His day had been busy and he's glad the weekend has arrived. I tell him to enjoy it then, and he replies I am really sweet. *Hell, if only he knew what I was thinking . . .*

Of course, I can be sweet . . . but right now I started to fantasize about how Potential Hot Date #1 looked—for real, that is. Better meet-up fast so as not to be too disappointed . . . But, how to *(temporarily, of course)* reject on behalf of lump without him losing interest?

This morning, I send him a video of a Cuban band, innocently asking whether this was maybe Old Blue Eyes' 'Singing in the rain' in Spanish. And I tell him to enjoy the weekend.

Potential Hot Date is of course not stupid, so he replies immediately, asking if I have time on Sunday evening. I inform him my eldest (who recently moved out) is coming over for dinner, so better on either Monday or Thursday next week. But no dancing this time. *For, obviously, lump is still around . . . Grrrr . . .*

Monday it is! I'm so curious, and even more nervous . . .

Either it's 'meet my stalker' time or . . . what else? *Yeah, yeah, Clooney is definitely sexy as well; but as my taste in music, my taste in men is hugely diverse.*

Exciting . . . *loving mom and ex-business woman turning into sex-predator* . . . *Dangerous Woman* from Ariana Grande comes to mind.

Things do not happen.
Things are made to happen.

-John F. Kennedy

Monday, April 18th 2016
ALMOST THERE . . .

Another message from Potential Hot Date #1 at midday. Hopes I'm well, bon appétit, and looks forward to seeing me in the evening. I thank him and wish him bon appétit as well, and tell him 'see you later'.

Oh dear . . . if not my faithful lump, who is going to stop me?

When you start doubting your worthiness,
just know there is something only you can bring to the table.

Tuesday, April 19th 2016
HOT DATE #1, Part I

Came home a bit late . . . Potential Hot Date #1 from last night is now *a definite* Hot Date #1!

I call his number as soon as I arrive at the bar, and he is waiting for me outside. *How considerate! I couldn't imagine myself looking around for someone I didn't know in a place full of people.*

After preventing my jaw from dropping *(yes, THAT gorgeous)* and thinking, *hellloooo, breakfast!* I tell him I am extremely nervous, as this is a first for me, and I actually feel weird with the situation.

He says he is pleasantly surprised as well. *Scoring points already, Hot Date #1? Keep it coming!*

It would be so nice to be able to read minds at times like this—e.g., *It's a casual dating site, for God's sake, what do you expect?, or, Let's have a drink, and get the fuck out of here!*

Only these thoughts would not have cut it for me . . . Not really. Of course, I was after sex as well. I do have to remain honest here. But I have never been the kind of person to have sex with 'just anyone'. I have to be *very* attracted physically to someone. Or be drunk. I do need to feel the tingles. And not only physically. But it was even more than that for me today. It was also to feel 'appreciated' again. Wanted and desired. To be a woman . . . He would have to do a bit more than be just 'hot'. *Come on, Hot Date #1, I'm sure you've got it in you!*

And by God I swear, he is HOT *(yes, with capital letters)* and nice *and* interested . . . *and, and, and . . .* Oh yeah, and honest as well. About the girlfriend who couldn't keep up with him sexually *(Really? Do I actually need/wanna hear this now?)*, his kids, his home country, his family.

He asks about me and my projects, and he seems genuinely interested. Always makes me slightly suspicious, though, having lived around someone who would throw it all back in my face at one point or another.

He's a master seducer, his actions working purely on instinct; and I do feel as if I already knew him. A thought I had not yet finished, when he said it out loud. *Weird* . . .

But hell, after a Cuba Libre and a cigarette, and a kiss outside the bar (*Mmm . . . heaven! The lips, I mean, not the cigarette*), I was left with even more confrontational issues.

For fuck's sake! I'm a '*Femme du Monde*', an ex-multi-million company owner ... and I have a communication problem on a date?! *Why?!*

But, honestly . . . at 49, how do you tell someone he's hot and you want him (without being considered 'cheap' or a 'predator' or worse)? Even more so because I am still a married woman. Is this considered cheating? Does this make me like every single cheating woman in the world? Because that is not the impression I want to leave. Not even on a 'casual date' . . . *You see, I told you I am not the casual type; I think too much.* I had fought for a lost cause for many years before I even considered doing what I am doing right now . . . *Why is this important for me? Does he want to hear all this? Does he need to know all this?*

Eh, well . . . In short, I no longer know how to do this—I am at a loss. I've been out of the chase for so long. And to try to be my freakin' honest self is not easy when I am thinking too much and I am nervous . . .

Back inside after almost breaking my neck over the threshold (again, very Bridget-like), he orders us a mojito (*Nice one, Hot Date #1. It's my favorite!*), and I feel slightly drunk. I decide this is definitely my last drink if I wanna get back home in one piece—*with dear lump, of course* . . .

51

He sits next to me. Looks at me. Yep, something really hot and long-forgotten starts to burn right next to lump. He says he wants me. I try not to look around to see if someone is standing behind me. The small spots on my breasts start reacting as well, exactly when he takes my hand and draws me to him to dance.

Mmmm, all muscle, and I feel (literally) that I am wanted . . . At my age, am I after all still being considered 'hot'?—*Haaa! Point to self!*

We step outside for another cigarette, and I decide to be honest about my Bridget-like escapade with the shaving and lump as a result. He laughs, tells me I'm funny, but doesn't seem to care about lump. I stress the fact that lump is really noticeable. No reaction to lump, but lips on mine. *Mmmm . . . language barrier? Who cares. lump doesn't speak anyway.* And I haven't had sex in almost 1.5 years.

Back in the bar, I have a coffee and we're making out in public. Wow, I feel like a teenager. He tells me again he wants me. *Whoa! Steady, nipples!*

We go out for a walk downtown, kiss, talk some more, then pick up my car to drive him home where he invites me in for a coffee (*Yeah, right*). I was at a loss. Me at 49 . . . a sex goddess? Wanted by this extremely handsome man?

Aïe, aïe, and aïe . . .

Sex with Hot Date #1 is a marathon - timewise and exercise wise. Ok, now know why his girlfriend may have a problem with this. Not everyone is cut out for long (*I mean really, really long*) hot sex.

But considering I actually DID run a marathon and still have the endurance, I recover fast, *and* I haven't had sex in almost 1.5 years, I do not really mind. Quite the contrary. Not to mention the fact that I am definitely a Capricorn and he is there being so extremely sexy.

But how will a future Hot Date #2 measure up to that?

And how is it possible to have done without sex this long?

Note to self: Go and find sex-proof eye make-up, as I now look like a panda . . .
Definitely not sexy.

PS: He seems to have enjoyed it as well, by the way . . . 😊

The worst guilt is to accept an unearned guilt.

-Ayn Rand

Wednesday, April 20 2016
WHAT NEXT?

In the meantime, I am being pursued by another guy *(no, not from the dating site)* whom I am definitely NOT interested in. So I tell him I am not a 'free' woman, but if he's interested in having a drink, talking, and laughing, we could go out some time. He doesn't reply. *If only he knew, hahaha.*

Follow-up on Hot Date #1:

Upon getting in my car after the first marathon, a message comes in straight away: 'Thank you for your visit. It was extremely beautiful. Sleep well. Hope to see you again.' *Exactly my thoughts, Señor. It was sooooo decidedly nice.*

I send back a kissing smiley and leave it at that. I also leave my phone in the car upon arriving home, but I can't be bothered going back to fetch it. I am comatose, and only wake up a couple of hours later.

I get up to walk the dog. Tired, but with a huge smile on my face. Thoughts whirling through my mind. And the nipple feeling every time I think of what happened. Yeah, what DID happen? It felt like Señor was there late last night and early morning just to please me, right? Oh, right, and please he did, and please do it again. I want more . . .

Car drivers in the town I live in are extremely polite. As I am about to cross the road, a man stops his car to give me right of way. While crossing, he opens his window and says, "Good exercise walking the dog in the morning." I turn to look at him and just smile at him sheepishly—*could he have read my bloody mind?*

Back home, I send a message to Hot Date #1 to tell him (shyly) about the car driver. Hot Date #1 immediately replies that yes, probably the car driver had noticed 'something'—did you sleep well?—enjoy your day.

Now THAT came unexpected. Does he really care? Or is he only being polite? Is it an 'age' thing? I remember from my roaring youth that sometimes we wouldn't even get back to someone after a wild night, or at least not till we were interested in a second date. But then again, we didn't have mobile phones in those years.

I reply at once that I had been wasted and getting up had been hard; tell him I feel 'whole', and that this is meant as a compliment. I ask him how he feels. He replies at midday that in the morning he had been reasonably fit, but after lunch he had also felt a little KO. I let him know I didn't think I would be productive that day.

And I wasn't. I am all conflicted about the affair. How is it possible to have had an affair and not feel guilty? Am I such a bad person? Every time I think about what I've done with Hot Date #1, my nipples tighten, and I'm contracting down-under. This goes on pretty much all day.

Does this lack of guilt mean that all the feelings I once had for my husband are completely gone? After all the fighting and manipulating and trying to communicate, to change things to get our marriage back on track, was it now finally beyond saving? A harsh reality. One I think I've known for a long time, only wanting it to be different. But there you have it.

At the end of the day, he asks me about my productivity, to which I reply that I'm dreaming. A kissing smiley in return. Me, being my bold self, tell him, 'Me cabeza en las nubes' (My head is in the clouds, according to Google Translate, that is.) He asks me to write in English - but did understand my Spanish. Later that evening, he wishes me a good night and sweet dreams, and hopes I'm fit again in the morning. *Why? Got plans, Hot Date #1?*

But I didn't get that message till Wednesday morning, as I was already off to dreamland. I text him the minute I wake up (*and that's quite something, 'cause to have me do anything at all before my café au lait in the morning is highly unusual).*

He says, 'Buenos Días', and sends me a 1000 kisses. *That gives me the nipple feeling again.* I simply send him a shy smiley.

Same evening, he asks me how my day was . . .

Yeah . . . how was my day?

Now that I am reasonably rational again *(am I?),* I try to analyze my feelings, but I have a hard time doing this. I don't want to give everything spontaneously, as I have been hurt by 'giving it all' before. But by not being spontaneous, I am not me. If I am spontaneous and my freakin' honest self, do I come across too aggressively? It's a dilemma I cannot—do not want to—resolve, not now. I cannot change for anyone or anything without losing myself, and I was lost already somewhere in the middle before, right? All this doesn't make sense to me . . . Me, on an 'affair' trip. But what does? And, do I actually not feel guilty? That is an emotion I am scared of, as I have felt guilty for the last 8 years. Guilty for existing. For not living up to expectations. Pushed off my pedestal. And if that were not enough, I have felt stepped on as well.

Nope, no guilt to be found. And I cry. Not because I am sad—on the contrary . . . I am finally free, and it feels wonderful, and I am in love. No, *NOT* with Hot Date #1. I am in love with myself and with life!

I do feel liberated . . . at last !

I decide that my projects will continue progressing in the background, but I need to get out of the home situation ASAP. Get a job, find a house, and have fun. Facebook friend was right.

I'm on a mission . . .

So I write him back. *Hola, ¿qué tal? (that's correct, at least.)* I tell him I have trouble concentrating, and it's driving me nuts.

He writes that maybe I need a massage, and his door is always open for me. I tell him that he must be kidding, for that would never calm me down. I mention that if the kids were not at home, I would have jumped in the car right away to find out. He proposes to meet on Friday. Where? His place, of course. Mmmm, dangerous. Dangerous is nice, and can I find the place? Sure I can—I was not actually that drunk on Monday. Nervous, though. Shall I bring food? No, I can make do *(and I'm thinking: yes, please do me, and there goes the nipple feeling again)*. I'd like that, Señor. Kissing smiley.

I who have died am alive again today,
and this is the sun's birthday;
this is the birthday of life

-e e cummings

Thursday, April 21st 2016
WALKING THE DOG …

> "Good morning. Did you sleep well? Enjoy your day. 😊 🐺"
>
> "Aïe, señor . . . Wild dreams . . . Did you sleep well? Enjoy your day too! 😗"
>
> "Yes, I dreamed about you. Thank you." *(thank me for what? what did I do to you in your dreams? mmmmm wish I was having that same dream too).*

The weather is as beautiful as I feel, and I take a picture from the lakeside, which I send to Hot Date #1, saying, "Buenos días."

Every day, when I walk the dog by the lakeside, I come across a jogger (*Not bad, either. Why is it I see 'not bad, either' guys all over the place lately?*), and he always looks at me in a very serious way. *Maybe he's scared of my dog?* Today, I decide I have had enough. *Either you jog or you talk!*

So when the jogger arrives and looks me in the eye, I say good morning. His eyes widen slightly (*Surprise? Nice eyes, btw*), but he does reply with a 'Good morning'. OK, that's a start . . . and not a minute later he joins me at the traffic light on my way back home. Now I keep a steady pace when walking the dog, so he jogs slowly beside me and starts to talk. Nice, a jogging stalker.

For the time being, I have enough to handle with Hot Date #1. But hope starts growing in me that perhaps we do not need the discomfort of dating sites. That maybe you could meet new people just by being friendly and slightly bold? Or am I kidding myself? The couple of single (women) friends I have keep telling me that it's a war zone . . . Why do I feel it different today?

Nice 'son' story on the 'good morning' subject.

A couple of weeks back when walking the dog with my son, he remarked, "Mom, do you know all these people?" We've only lived here for a year, you see. I replied that no, I did not. He then asked, "Then why do you say hello to all these people?"

'If someone looks at me, I would feel really uncomfortable not saying anything.' He said that I was radiating, and that made people wanna look at me. And that he was sure that within another year, everyone on that road I walked daily would say 'Hi!' to each other because I did that. I had to swallow a tear. *Sweet sensitive boy*. If only it were that simple . . .

Hot Date #1 writes me back that he enjoyed the picture. I have no time to think about him anymore—need to be productive. Send him a kissing smiley. But nipples disagree . . .

At midday, he wishes me *bon appétit*, so I tell him about the homemade lunch I prepared, and let him know that I have to go to a language course in the evening, but could think of something better to do (with a shy smiley). I ask him how his lunch was. God, he needs to stop with this messaging—I can't concentrate, I can't eat, and I wake up in the middle of the night from sweet dreams. I definitely do not want to be a sex-crazed bitch, do I? Nymphomania comes to mind briefly. Do I have a choice? Must be menopause playing with me . . . Hahaha. Let your hair down! Enjoy while you can!

He had a nice lunch as well, and do not worry, we'll meet tomorrow night, and do I eat spicy? I ask him to define spicy. *If it's Cuban and naked, I'll have it.* Instead, I say that I do like spicy, but I need a drink with it. He tells me to bring the drinks then. I ask him what he wants to drink, and he says that he's got what he needs, but if I like anything else than rhum, I should bring that to enjoy. I tell me water would be all I need (so as *not to dehydrate any more than necessary*). He tells me I'm sweet, and I write back that I received a message once that said, *If life throws lemons at you, instead of making a sour face, you'd better ask for Tequila & Salt to go with it.* I guess that his rhum would do as well. He tells me he is excited to meet me tomorrow, and is now off downtown with colleagues. I tell him to enjoy.

Later in the evening, I write him that I am sad because Prince died. So many sweet memories to go with his songs. I strongly believe that everything in this world is somehow related. People, memories, songs, movies, theatre, places, dreams—everything!

A bit later, he replies that he'd read that as well, and that it is too bad. *That's it? I feel disappointed that it's just 'too bad' for him, as I felt so much more. But of course, I didn't tell him more than 'I'm sad,' either, so . . .*

Hasta mañana, lover boy. Not even my good ole lump could stop me from going back there.

Don't dress to kill.
Dress to survive

-Karl Lagerfeld

Friday, April 22nd 2016
HOT DATE #1, Part II

"Good morning, beautiful, are you ok? Did you sleep well?"

Again the weather is so beautiful, and reflections on the lake are extraordinary, so I send him another picture, telling him that no, I didn't sleep that well. What about him? Enjoy your day. Kissing smiley.

He didn't sleep well, either—woke up at 003h00. Tells me to enjoy lunch.

This is getting spooky . . . On a first date, he speaks my thoughts; ok, it can happen. But waking up at the same time because we're both not sleeping well? Mmmm, let's see what happens next.

In the afternoon, I meet up with the girls, as we have a 50th birthday coming up. We will be dressing up for the occasion in the birthday girl's local traditional dress, and we modified a song with text that applies to all our escapades. Having a lots of fun. But I also have a hard time suppressing my slumbering feelings, for they actually *do* notice something (*the stupid grin on my face, maybe?*), and start asking questions. Was I dressed up only for the vernissage I was headed to after our meet-up? Or was there something else I wasn't saying? *Mmmmm, sweet secret . . . Will have to tell them someday . . . But not now!*

I head off to the vernissage.

Text to Hot Date #1 that I am running late. He writes back, "No stress, I'm here." Hell, I'm nervous . . . *Why? Because you now 'know' what you're gonna do, babe. This is soooooo not me. Yeah, but you want it anyway, right?* Right.

And there he is. All of him . . . Shit, my whole body just tightens up at the sight of this man. Have you ever been deprived of sex for 1.5

years? Well, this is pretty much how you feel and react when you 'wake up'. *No more waiting, Señor. Do me now.*

He asks if I am hungry (*Sí, señor, for more sex*), and I reply, 'Not too much.' He tells me I need to eat for energy. (*Sí, señor, I'll eat you.*) I agree. So he cooks.

I watch, feeling like a feline ready to attack, and at the same time like prey, as I now know what is coming. He fixes me a Cuba Libre to unwind (*doesn't work on me, by the way*) which I enjoy, but his lips are far more enjoyable. *Mmmm, he's stalling for time? Teasing? Can't read him right now. Having contractions.*

OK, summarize (*while Hot Date #1 is cooking*) . . . I meet a guy on the internet, see him for the first time 1.5 weeks later, and after two weeks I'm almost drooling with want? WTF? Get real, babe! But being my spontaneous self, I just can't. I simply have to find out what this is all about! A new me is on the loose. Or is it a younger me coming out again?

I try to pull myself together, but when not able to be myself, I become nervous, and words don't come out the way I plan . . .

While kissing and groping, he says it all goes so fast (*not fast enough, hon—get on with it!*), and he talks about not falling in love. *From far away, alarm bells start ringing. Stop! Did I hear this right? Falling in love? Who is falling in love? Is he talking about me? About him?* Not sure whether I understood well, I tell him rather soberly that I do whatever the fuck pleases me, and that was the end of the conversation. Later, I thought maybe we should have talked about this, because, well, honestly, I don't want to let go of my new-found pleasure in being a woman again. And after all, I was extremely rude, and he did look a bit astonished by my outburst. *Am I coming on too strong? Do I want too much, too soon? But too much of what? He was the one who said his girlfriend couldn't handle the relation on the sexual front. Let ME have it, then, hombre . . .*

And I did. 2 marathons in one week? I feel like a living legend of a sex goddess!

In between, we DID have dinner. *Vaya, a man who can cook!* While eating, we covered a diversity of topics. This telepathic relation he has with his mom. His two brothers. Music. Voodoo. I tell him I believe everything plays out as it is meant to. I am convinced I have lived different lives. *How else can I be so attracted to towns that I have never before visited in my (current) life?* I know things without remembering how and where I learnt them. I 'see' and 'feel' spirits. So does he. So much in common. I still do not know what he does for a living. That's for another time. Dessert?

We have sex for dessert. Another thing in common. An extremely healthy appetite for special desserts.

He asks me to stay over, but I don't. Through all my young wild years, I have never stayed over after one-night-stand sex. And those one-nighters definitely never ever happened at my house. What does this tell about me? *Suzy Homemaker doesn't want any mess around her house, but if it's at someone else's house … is that ok?* Only 'friends with benefits' were allowed in. There has been quite a number of those as well. I think maybe I have to feel 'in love' one way or another to be able to wake up next to someone. Or at least be highly attracted to the person. On a personal or spiritual level, that is.

I might stay over one day, though I doubt it. Hot Date #1 may look like a potential 'friend with benefits'. But not now, and definitely not after the 'falling in love' thingie. It will take me a bit more (*a lot, actually*) to be in love again after all the unhappy years. But in the end, it's all everyone needs, right? Being in love, being loved. However, I so do like the 'loving' I receive right now.

I have to be careful not to let my sex drive overtake me. And why's that? Oh, fuck it, just enjoy the ride!

Back in the car, I receive a message, wishing me nice dreams, and hoping to see me soon. I send him back a kissing smiley.

If you want to run,
run a mile.
If you want to experience a different life,
run a marathon.

-Emil Zatopek

Saturday, April 23rd 2016
MUSE?

Text him I just woke up (*at midday!*) and I'm feeling good. Tell him to enjoy the weekend, as he told me last night he was going to be out of town (*the girlfriend?*)

He replies he's getting ready to go—did I sleep well?—and he will message me when he is back on Monday.

I tell him I had sweet dreams this time. Did he sleep well? Also, I inform him I'd only be lazy and do nothing today. After all, lazy people are creative people, right? Wish him a nice weekend again.

He tells me he slept extremely well, and sends me a kissing smiley.

I seem to have quiet and sweet dreams after a sex marathon with Hot Date #1, but on other days, I have wild dreams and I wake up soaked—somebody please give me an explanation!

I write him my jeans are too large.

I have never been one to check on my weight regularly, as I will immediately feel it in my jeans and belt. So now, time to get on those scales again?

Right. After two marathons with Hot Date #1, my jeans start becoming baggy. WTF? That's all it takes? But yes, I remember when training for the NYCM (*the real thing, I mean*), I was eating anything that came in sight, and I was still losing weight. I bet today I could close jeans I bought back then.

This afternoon, when waiting for the elevator to take me down, my neighbor and friend comes out and smiles at me. She looks at me from head to toe, and says, 'Gal, you look like sex on legs!' *Haaaa—if only you knew* . . .

I feel raw, tired, as if I had had sex all night *(well, I did a big part of the evening and night)*. And I'm feeling good . . . lazy, raw, but good.

'Feeling Good' from Muse plays in my mind . . .

The desire of the man is for the woman,
but the desire of the woman is for the desire of the man.

-Madame de Stael

Sunday, April 24th 2016
BLOODY SUNDAY

"Señor, tengo un problema . . . Today I had 3 cold showers and a 30-minute run . . . Now what?"

"Hi, sorry. Was out of town." *(I know, estupido)* "Driving home now. What, did you drink that much?"

"Nada. Nothing at all"

"Ok, I misunderstood 😨."

"You ok? Did you have a nice w/end?"

"Yes, all was good, and you? Am in the train now. Kiss."

"Quiet, did girls' things with my daughter. Masks, hair, make-up."

Nothing further. No text in return . . . Guess if he says I'll get back to you on Monday, it means he'll get back to me on Monday. Aww, someone please explain the rules to me! I am going mad. I want to be wanted yet once more. Plain desire is what I need, and right now! This man is making me feel like a nymphomaniac.

I guess I'll have another cold shower. Sunday, bloody Sunday, it is!

Learn the rules like a pro,
so you can break them like an artist

-*Pablo Picasso*

Monday, April 25th 2016
FORCED

The morning promenade was refreshing. Cold but beautiful, with the promise of a glorious day. I send Hot Date #1 a picture of the sun behind the clouds with a *Buenos Días* from here.

He writes me back with a *Ciao, Bella, Buenos Días, and how are you?*

Mmmmm. I tell him about my neighbor calling me 'sex on legs' and my friend calling me radiant, so I guess I was OK. Are you?

> "Wow . . . yeah, all is fine."
>
> "Meet for coffee?"
>
> "No, no time" (*WTF*)
>
> "OK—*what do I reply to that?*"
>
> "😘😊" (*that's hopeful 'cause not interested in more cold showers nor running*)
>
> "What about tonight?"
>
> "Today is not good. I have a long training program *(yeah, go for it!—make that body even more beautiful)*, but tomorrow would be superb." With a kissing smiley. *(Can I wait that long? Maybe it's time to find a Hot Date #2?)*
>
> "Will try to arrange—let you know later." Kissing smiley.

With the intention of not replying, of course . . . What the hell is he thinking? What the hell am *I* thinking? Hot Date #1 has been in my life for a week, 'live' that is, and two marathons further he has to be at my beck and call? That's not fair, is it? Oooohh, but I hate those cold showers . . .

3 hours later . . .

"I'll be finished by 20h30, if it's not too late for you. But we can't make it very long" (*a half-marathon? Kidding, right, it's all or nothing, hon*). "Haha. 😵"

"You'll probably be tired after training. 😊"

"Probably. 😵"

I didn't bother to reply. I went for a run. That would bring me back to reality. Yeah, right . . . When you are running, you just think, as there is nothing else to do. Did I mention I hate running? Yes, the NYC marathon runner does hate running. To me, it's all in the challenge . . . *Hang in there, Hot Date #1!*

I mean, he's kidding, right? I've been wanting and waiting for more since early Saturday morning when I left his apartment. Why can he not be an asshole? At least I would not have to be nice. Then again, I probably wouldn't have wanted more either. Oh, fuck the hormones! Could it be that I am secretly wanting something more monogamous? I have never before been in a situation like this. Where is the manual when you need it ?

Fact #1—I met Hot Date (still #1) through a casual dating site.

Fact #2—I wanted attention, fun, going out, to be desired, and hot sex.

Fact #3— We've been open about our personal lives. *I'm still married; he has a girlfriend.*

Fact #4—Expectations—that is still open, isn't it? Mine are clearly fact #2, but his? What does he want from all this? Just sex?

Maybe there are no rules? Perhaps we have to make up our own rules as we go along? But then we have to be clear, right? We've been honest about our personal lives. But have we been clear enough about our

75

expectations?

'Cause honestly, I would have been on his doorstep every freakin' night since we first met—that's how much I am in need of being desired. But I do enjoy the attention of his texting; it's sort of online seducing to me. Something completely new in my life, but if this counts as an expectation, it wouldn't be as nice anymore, right?

Shit, I will have to talk about the 'falling in love' red flag with him—that's actually really bugging me.

Conclusion: I do not need him to be monogamous—he may have and enjoy his girlfriend. What is frustrating is that I realize I want '*it*' to happen when *I* want it. *Easy there, don't spoil his appetite.*

> "Sorry, was out for a run . . . It was either running or being frustrated 😁 You woke up my body and it's a bit" *(a lot)* out of control . . . Either tonight or tomorrow. (If the latter, I'll have to torture myself with cold showers again), or both . . . 😊"
>
> "Ok, let's leave it for tomorrow. Big kiss."
>
> "Ok, torture it is—payback time tomorrow 😌"
>
> "Yes, sure 😗 Now I will have a shower. 😖"
>
> "Cold, please 😁 😁"
>
> "Hahaha. Are you already home?"
>
> "Yes, was in town all day."
>
> "Ok, let's wait till tomorrow. 😊" *(he's leading me on, right?)*
>
> "Pfffff old man 😝"
>
> "Hahaha. You can come over now if you want. 😌" *(hahaha, he doesn't like to be called old)*
>
> "Don't tease—my hormones are completely fucked up—they

76

don't understand what's happening to them, but they want more 😳"

"Hahaha, all right I'm here, going for a shower now." *(pictures in my mind: Hot Date #1 in the shower . . . mmmm)*

"21h00-21h15"

"Ok 😙 Have nothing to drink, only Martini. 😊 😗"

"Water?" *(better against dehydration while having wild sex)*

"Good 😊"

"Want me to bring something? Can stop @ the gas station."

"No."

Doubt

Tuesday, April 26th 2016
HOT DATE #1, Part III

I feel wonderful, beautiful, and awkward all at the same time. Beautiful and wonderful because I had extremely nice-and-hot sex last night. But awkward because I still have this issue of the 'falling in love' remark at the back of my mind. Somehow, last night, after a half-marathon (still nice, but less intense), it was not the right time to bring it up. Not to mention the fact that I forced myself into this third date. Not good.

And I believe that grinning stupidly and asking, '*Wot?*' isn't going to do it for him *(not for me, anyway)* in the long run. If there is any long run, that is. And my intuition tells me there is doubt.

For the time being, I am so much better writing it all down. I am afraid to express my feelings to him, as that would make it a 'relationship,' wouldn't it? Can you be a 'couple' with one person and have a 'relationship' with another? How do people having affairs do this? How does it work? Maybe I'll ask Hot Date #1, as he's an expert on cheating on his girlfriend! But I am still looking at it as a married woman, and this may be what's wrong with my whole point of view. Yes, by law I am still married, but in reality I no longer am. Am I 'casual dating' material? Or do I need something more? The 'friend with benefits'? I am no longer 17, nor 25 . . . so stop beating about the bush and get on with it. And in the meantime . . . ENJOY!

Message from Hot Date #1 upon leaving last night:

> "Thank you for your visit, drive safely and sleep well. Was nice. Very."

With lots of kissing smileys.

One kissing smiley back. That's enough, he doesn't deserve more than one after only half a marathon.

Next morning is a wild morning. The lake is extraordinary, just the way I feel—extraordinary after sleeping with Sex-god, and wild because my mind is turbulently seeking answers I most probably won't find today. I have to let go and live the moment. I send Hot Date #1 a picture of my wild lake, with a caption "wild morning."

"Hey, Buenos días, did you sleep well? Wild but beautiful."

"Hola, Señor ☺, very nice & quiet sleep. You? Thank you for having me (*always stay polite . . . and after all he did have me*). Feel more comfortable now (*of course I do, sex instead of cold shower, much better, right?*). Enjoy your day 😘"

"Gracias, here all ok (*does he ever become tired?*). A lot of work. Enjoy your day 😘"

"Chasing my dreams ☺ Talk later 😗"

At 12h00

"Bon appétit, hope you are ok 😗"

"No lunch today, having a coffee and apple by the PC. Talk about website development. Whether to have it done for a lot of money or try it myself first. Before deciding on options I have a meet with 2 students who may be interested in doing it as a school project. Was your morning ok? Talk later 😘"

At 17h00

"Here all ok, gracias, am glad the day is over 😗"

"Rest. You ok, handsome? Just finished work."

"Cool, I'll jump in the shower. Gracias for calling me handsome." (*shower? handsome? Hey, I'll have that for breakfast, lunch, and dinner anytime*) "You're sweet 😘"

"Sometimes yes, sometimes no 😷 Buenos Noches marathon-lover ☺"

"Hello, Bella, go to bed early" *(what, you? or me? or together? mmmmm)* "sleep well and 1000 kisses there where you like them most" (*now I will definitely not be able to sleep*)
"Tomorrow 😜"

"Nipples going wild 😊 Sweet dreams . . ."

Sorry for my bluntness,
that's just how I roll ...

-Cannabis Sativa

Wednesday, April 27th 2016
PHILOSOPHY

I can't stop thinking I am coming on too strong, too aggressive—but hey, I am only just starting the 'game'. No one explained the rules, so . . . take it or leave it!

I recently woke up from the living dead, and I want to enjoy it some more. *Hot Date #1, you woke me up, so I feel it's your responsibility to give it to me.*

This is how I am . . . No rules, no limits, and say what you want, whenever you want it—although I must admit, it's hard to speak my thoughts when I'm trembling in Hot Date's presence, as I know what's coming to me.

I asked Hot Date once or twice what I should do to please him, and he told me, "You please me." Helllloooo, nipples . . .

I feel a bit philosophical this morning, so I send him a short text to read:

> "We are taught to count seconds, minutes, hours, days, years . . .
> But no one explains to us the value of a moment."

Does the value of a moment need explaining? Is this not rather more of a 'feeling' than a 'value'? Well, maybe, but definitely not in Casual Dating World, I believe. There's no value to casual dating other than a temporary fulfilment. No feelings.

Later on, he writes that he agrees with that, and wishes me *bon appétit*.

I reply that this was enough philosophy for the day *(After all, it was already midday)*, but I do like to reflect on either a text or an image *(hence, a picture a day*) to start off the day, and, lately that image was of a godly body. "Have a wonderful afternoon. Smiley."

Hot Date #1 writes me back at the end of the afternoon that it was beautiful. He is lying down in bed for a while (*God, did he have to put that image in my head? Nipples, right?*), and he asks me if I'm OK.

Yeah, sure, seeing Sex-god in bed makes me feel all right . . . So I tell Señor to not place pictures in my head, that I'm off to town, and can we speak later?

See if Estée Lauder can help me with some sex-proof make-up . . . How am I going to bring THAT to the saleswoman?

I text him later to find out how his day has been. He was dead tired, wanted to go dancing (*mmm yeah, I'd like to dance with Hot Date #1*), but had an early start next day, so not even time for sex. (*Another picture comes to mind.*)

> "No worries, hombre, need to rest, and although hype & raw, I still want more. Just being honest, hombre. I'll leave you to it."
>
> "I want you too, honey, but want to have you very slowly . . ." *(contractions . . . omg and he's only texting . . .)*
>
> "Aaargh, no teasing, please . . . Can't handle it right now. I do need to call in an early night, and your teasing will stop me from being able to sleep 😬"
>
> "What do you like the most, what is your fantasy?" *(fuck me now, Señor, I'm sooo ready . . .)*
>
> "Aïe—at this moment, you naked in my bed. 😊" *(see how easy to please I am?)* "Nipples leading their own life again, which makes my stomach tighten . . . Want you, hombre 😊"

He then tells me it's training time. *Oh yeah, keep that muscle coming, hon.*

Have a good one, you perturbing macho-man.

Yep, it's end of April and it has been snowing today. With the philosophical reflections of the day, Red Hot Chili Peppers' 'Snow' says it all . . .

I wish I was full of chocolate gateau instead of feelings ...

-Jim Bugg

Thursday, April 28th 2016
HOT DATE #1, Part IV

This morning, I found a serving tray with an empty glass on it on a rock on the lake side. I took a picture, and sent it to Hot Date saying someone had either had a late night or an early breakfast. "Enjoy your day, sexy. Kissing smiley."

Later on, he replies that maybe it was me? And maybe we could see each other tonight?

I tell him no, it wasn't me. I was too busy thinking of wild sex with a sexy Cuban. Tell him would love to come (*really* . . .) but have language class tonight—maybe tomorrow?

> "Hola, chica. No, tomorrow not possible. If not tonight, then Sunday?"
>
> "Do I wanna wait that long?" *(Nahhh . . .)*
>
> "I could skip class for once 😌 What time? Where?"
>
> "Heeee . . . my place, 20h00 😌" *(sí, Señor)*
>
> "Señor, you knock me off my feet 😳"
>
> "Hahaha—see you later 😊" *(not even an earthquake could stop me!)*
>
> "I won't do dinner *(he can have me instead, right?)*, but will bring dessert, you like chocolate?"
>
> "I am chocolate, you may bring something to drink 😊"
>
> "Yeah, hahaha, 'hot' chocolate 😛 I'll bring both."

Now, *my* chocolate gateau is known as a chocolate orgasm, for it's soft and mushy on the inside and hard and crusty meringue on the outside, and the taste is just divine . . . Hope I'm not fucking it up. I'm trembling with anticipation.

Writes me he's already home, time to relax. Am I OK? *(Am I? Really?)*

Mmmmm . . .

Off for a shower, leave the shaving to men. I'll wax next week.

Sexual pleasure is a legitimate right of the human being ...

-Samael Aun Weor

Friday, April 29th 2016
HONEST(L)Y ...

He does need his beauty sleep on weeknights! Again, a half-marathon. This morning, when getting on the scales, I noticed that I had lost 5.6 kg since January, and I can tell you it was approximately -1 kg when I met my FB friend earlier this month. So, 4.5 kg in one-and-a-half weeks? Really? Not only good for the mind—my Hot Date #1—but also for my body ... I want more of all that! *Hey, what diet are you on? I'm on the Cuban diet. Really? What's that? Oh, nothing special. I have a Cuba Libre every night, then think of a hot Cuban so that I feel sexy and I am no longer hungry. So very sexy, that only thinking about it makes me lose weight.*

Message as I get in the car:

> "Sweet dreams, and thanks a lot for your visit. See you soon. Pssss ... I like you 😘"

WTF—this is skin-crawling, earth-moving, and oh-so-exciting sex! On top of that, Hot Date #1 is a cool, considerate, handsome, and sexy man. *Or a master seducer.* Whatever ... I am having a good time! Could he be 'friend with benefits' material? Via a casual dating site? Mmmm ...

Anyway, as I enter his apartment and he fixes me a drink, I am led by the hand and told there is a present waiting for me. *For real? Aww, sweet!*

And sweet sexy it was, my present: the relaxing (*yeah, right!*) massage he had promised by text last week. After more intense exercising, we sit down over a drink, and Hot Date #1 is eating my chocolate orgasm (*haaa!*) and says he should marry me. I choke on my Cuba Libre ... *WTF, come again?* I reply I am not interested in boyfriend material, and

90

now that he mentions this—we need to talk. He says, "Here we go." *What was he expecting?* So I finally brought up the 'in-love' issue (almost a week later), and said I didn't know what he meant. Was he talking about me? Was he talking about himself? I also tell him I'm sorry for having reacted so strongly, but that my new-found freedom and obvious 'need' for more had made me lose control. *Yeah, right! Blame it on the hormones!* He said he had been talking about both of us, that everything went so fast. *Well, he shouldn't be such a hunk then! Wouldn't be back for more if he weren't that edible!*

I reassured him again I wasn't jealous. I didn't mind him having a girlfriend because, after all, isn't she the reason I am here? *But could I deal with him having another sex partner? Mmm, have to think about that one, and maybe discuss this at a later time.* I tell him again that I definitely do not want a boyfriend at this stage of my life. *And would I want him as a boyfriend ever? What with the way we met? So easy to do to me what he is doing to his girlfriend, even though she may not be aware. But how to trust someone whom you know to be in such need of physical action?* But, the one thing that *is* crucial to me is that he is honest with me. And straightforward. Either yes or no, no maybes. Either you want me like that or you don't. Heavenly lips on mine. OK, that's an answer to please Señor.

We talk some more about our private situations, and he tells me he has been with his current girlfriend for 7 years. I thought I was going to fall off my chair. Seven bloody years? He explains that she is perfect in every way. She is always there for him. She's beautiful. They travel. She listens without judgment, and she is fun to be with. *So much fun that I've just got panda-faced by Hot Date #1?* But she doesn't have the same appetite for sex as he does. *Hell, why be with someone if you're not happy with the sex to start with?*

And I feel sorry for Hot Date #1. I do. And for the girlfriend as well. What a punishment to be having a LAT relation with someone who is compatible in almost everything, but not there when the going gets

91

tough, and you need him the most. Apparently, she wants him to move in with her, but he's used his kids, who live close by, as an excuse to rule out that option. Sad. Guess we cannot all live a life like Christian Grey, who has it all exactly the way he wants it . . .

You see, I now find myself luckier than I thought with my situation. I *know* we are finished, the almost-ex and me. I *can* move on without a grudge. On a clean slate. No reproaches to be made any longer. But what if I now fall into the same category as Hot Date #1? What if, in the future, I find a man who is perfect in many ways, but not in bed? Would I be willing to compromise? Comparisons have started. Hot Date #1 vs. *all* of my past boyfriends. There's one I can think of who was a lot of fun being with. Another one who bought me nice things. Yet another one who wined & dined me. And a lot I only had sex with. I lost count. And out of all these men (boys/young men at the time), there's only one I can think of I really enjoyed on all levels. And he didn't move to please . . . so that also became boring after a while (it's not the size, but the intention to please).

Hot Date #1, I now officially hate you for having allowed me to meet you.

Anyway, I demand to know how he can hold his climaxing for so long. Believe me, it is rare. With all the information we have access to today, tantric practices are not the ones sought after. As mentioned before, I've been with a 'few' men in my life, and *never ever* have I met a man with this kind of endurance.

He replies, as he holds my face, that the more I am excited and seemingly pleased, the more he is excited and the longer he wants to keep the pleasure 'high.' *My Hot Date #1 has inhuman tantric endurance* . . .

Still over the same drink, I say, 'I asked you a couple of times what I can do to please *you*. 'Cause I still have the feeling you are here only to please *me* . . . Nothing's wrong, and I am definitely not complaining, but I want to please you the way you please me.' Shy smile.

Now THIS is what I'm talking about . . . We all know what we want and what we need, but somehow we're always afraid to ask for it! Isn't that just plain stupid?

So we talk about what pleases men in general (*him as well?—he didn't mention*). And we come to the subject of anal sex.

I take a deep breath. I did try it *(long ago)* on two occasions. The first time, I was drunk, and this left me with 1. diarrhoea, soon to be followed by 2. a week-long constipation *('cause it hurt so much),* and *(logic result)* 3. hemorrhoids *(aggravated by 3 pregnancies).* The second time, I tried it with my husband, but having been hurt on my initial attempt, I was not too 'hot' about it. He never asked for it again. But, of course, I didn't tell the Cuban Sex-god.

We talk some more. The ice is broken. I am more relaxed around him, and feel less of a need to continue holding back. I can be my freakin' rambling self! I smile. Time to go before I start all over on Cuban Hot Date #1 and go anal all by myself.

> "Like you too . . . Wild dreams . . . 😊"
>
> "Gracias 😊 😋"
>
> "De nada, hombre 😃 Gracias a toi"
>
> "Haha, a ti 😃"
>
> "Home safe—sweet dreams 😋"

Next morning:

> "Buenos días. Hope you slept well. You forgot your glasses. How do we do this? Do you have other glasses? Or do you need to pick them up today?" (*may I need those glasses*

93

today? Mmmmmm) "Tell me. Enjoy your day 😚"

"No worries, have more glasses 😊 Yes, slept like a baby—maybe need sex every day to rest well. Have fun today 😚"

"Ooooh no, please 😝"

"Can't handle it? Maybe I should consider taking an amant . . ."

"What do you mean with amant? 😊"

"Mmmmm lover in French . . ."

"Aha, Amante" *(yeah, hon, talk Spanish to me!)* "😌"

"In Spanish, but in French it is amant, which I find so much nicer than the English word 😊 Leaving with the dog . . . Happy we talked last night. The 'falling in love' issue was really bothering me 😗"

On my morning walk, nothing extraordinary as usual, but the spring light in the morning is so pretty. I take another picture of the landscape, and send it to Hot Date #1, saying, 'Glorious day, as beautiful as I feel. Thank you for making me feel good about myself.'

"😊 😚"

"Bon Appétit, are you ok? 😗"

"Mmmm, lying in the sun—feel like a lazy feline. Not hungry today, been living on coffee this morning, but should eat something at some stage. I'll have an apple as no kids for lunch today 😊 You had chocolate orgasm for breakfast? Are you ok, hombre? "

"Yes, I did 😊 Also enjoying the sun. Wish you a wonderful w/end. PS cannot write to you after tonight 😚"

"No worries—starting to learn 'the rules' 😌 😗"

"Enjoy your afternoon. "

"😖 😗"

Later in the afternoon:

"So finally w/end. Rest well" *(why, have something in mind, Señor?)*. "I'll get back to you on Sunday 😗 😗 😗"

"Enjoy your girls 😚"

"😊 😚"

Hotness is uniqueness.

And just being yourself ...
that's hot!

-Ryan Cabrera

Saturday, April 30th 2016

I HAD THOUGHT NO CONTACT OVER THE WEEKEND …

I run around like crazy all day as the apartment needs urgent cleaning. Lately, I just can't be bothered doing anything but vacuum cleaning— dust needs to get out . . . The only spotless space in our house is the kitchen, as I'm a maniac when it comes to my cooking and eating environment.

Also, I've been smoking like a chimney. Even more than usual. Eating is becoming a problem. I currently live on apples and crackers, and I force-feed myself with a little of whatever I'm fixing for the kids. I do take my vitamin supplements, though. I am not hungry. And I am dead tired, but at the same time I have a vitality I had long forgotten. Wow, hot sex is good for a lot of things, right?

After the cleaning, a quick coffee, then downtown for the neglected food shopping. Does this happen to you as well? Go food shopping for the weekend, but always forgetting this or that, and then having to return to the supermarket on a Saturday? I just hate it!

Then shower, make-up, dress, and off I go to the 50th birthday celebration of one of my 'unruly four' friends. Rendezvous at 17h00. I'm late *(it has now become a habit)* . . . I sing my throat out in the car like a madwoman. *Stop it! People are staring at you. Who cares? I'm happy!*

Wish Hot Date #1 could see me now, as I look like a million dollars, including stars in my eyes. "I Feel Good" (James Brown) is playing. Yeah, I feel good . . .

It was really nice to finally meet my friend's family. I've known her for almost 10 years, but had never met her parents and siblings. Besides her family, there were her in-laws, and three of her husband's friends.

Plus the three of us. Does she have any other friends besides us? Or did she make a choice not to invite everyone, as it was a sit-down dinner party? The food was delicious, and the company nice. I do hope she enjoyed what we prepared for her! Dressed in her local traditional dress, we sang her the song about all our escapades. She was laughing her head off, as was the whole room.

Did you know men go crazy over a Bavarian dress? They were drooling and grinning all over us after our silly performance. Apparently, they wanted us to spend the rest of the evening in these dresses. But I did not learn about that till a week later.

> "Ciao, Bella. How are you? What are you doing in this nice weather?" (*it was pouring down like there was no tomorrow*) "Kiss 😚"
>
> "Hola, hombre, am at my friend's 50th birthday party. Mainly older people. Luckily, the three maidens are here, gonna have fun after all . . . " (with a picture of the three of us singing in Bavarian dresses).
>
> "Ok, have fun. Hahaha 😚"
>
> "You're having fun too?"
>
> "Yeah, all good here 😊"

Ok, now what do I do with this . . . Hot Date #1 says no contact on the weekends, and now he texts me on a Saturday evening? What does he want? His daughters are over, aren't they? The party is slow, so I could leave early and see him. Actually, I AM wanting to see him, as I feel so 'alive'. But I don't tell him this. He needs to learn *(and fast)* that he has to be straight with me and tell me what he wants. Don't let matters open for interpretation (*at which I am a star—interpreting, that is*). Fuck Hot Date #1! I'm having fun! And I dance with his namesake, who's a clumsy dancer, clearly with the hots for me, but also clumsy and shy in his attitude. Poor guy was drooling . . . *I know how you feel, man. I really do.*

My soul met yours
and they instantly recognized each other
from many lives ago …

Sunday, May 1st 2016
JEWISH HUMOR?
Or did another soul sister just turn up . . .

Not a word from Hot Date #1. He had me 'interpret' that we may meet up on Sunday—but I guess he changed his mind. Oh well, I'm not going to be bothered today.

My voice has gone from the singing and laughing. My throat hurts 'cause I'd gone outside for a smoke on numerous occasions last night without putting on my jacket. I feel a cold coming up.

Now, when I talk about my soul sister, that is my local friend. She who knows all about me. My 'almost-ex' problems, my kids, my troubles, but also all the good times and, oh well, my everything. Including Hot Date #1. I lived through thick and thin with this woman for a good part of the last 20 years. We have a lot in common. Life approach, determination, values, strength, outgoing nature, laughter, and an easy-going attitude, to name a few. And the NYC Marathon, which brought us even closer. The sheer intensity of the training, and the marathon itself. The only real difference between us is the way we express ourselves towards the outside world. She is more of a politician and well-spoken; and I am, honestly, plain blunt.

But since early April, a potential new friend has turned up, and we are ALSO one of a kind. A completely different 'one of a kind'. Does this mean I have MPD? Nah . . . I've always had different 'kinds' of friends.

Is it because we speak the same language? Our directness and our manner of speech? No bullshit? We talk about our sexual escapades like men do. Open. Direct. And I guess we are, in a way. Men disguised as women? Nah, we're just very Dutch. Slightly more rude and honest in our language than a woman *should* be. But, of course, behaving like ladies when around other people. Naughty. But classy, nonetheless.

This Jewish pearl doesn't seem to care as long as she has sex with a penis. *But on the serious man-hunting side, she has her list of pre-requisites, of course.* Well, I believe you begin to understand. We enjoy the same drinks. Both 'gone wild' at age 49, same birth country, we understand each other's jokes where others don't. A large palette of similarities. Hell, we even have the same plates in the kitchen. Except for the sleeping with whomever. That I cannot. She can. She has me crying with laughter a good part of the Sunday with her latest escapade. We've texted a lot recently, and whenever the going gets 'peeing in my pants' tough, we call each other to laugh and cry out loud on the phone. I believe we must have been twins in a former life.

The 'almost-ex' is gone most of the day, and the kids will leave in the afternoon, so lazy Sunday for Mom it is . . .

The weekend is rainy and wet, but nice.

Emotions are not related to age
They are linked to a moment

We are ageless

Monday, May 2nd 2016
HOT DATE #1, Part V

Again, a beautiful morning with light that takes me to the moon and back. Is it an 'age' thing? The fact you can be so charmed just by looking at the light that shines on nature? Or is it the fact that you actually take the time to look around you? I don't seem to have had this when I was younger. Either you went to work early or you slept because you had been out the night before. So yes, maybe it is age-related after all.

Anyway, another picture sent to Hot Date #1.

> "Buenos días, Señor . . . Cómo estás this morning . . ."
>
> "Buenos, Bella, bien, gracias, y tú 😊 😗" (Aïe, Spanish . . . not good for nipples)
>
> "Too many cold showers 😊"
>
> "Still? 😬"
>
> "Mmmm I am in need 😊"

Later on:

> "Bon appétit 😊"
>
> "Thank you, you too. Are you training tonight or wanna meet? 😊 😗"
>
> "Hey honey, had a long day today, need to clean and train. Will be a bit late. Are you ok? 😗" (WTF—will be a bit late, but wants me there? or, will be a bit late—let's leave it for another time?)
>
> "Yeah, I'm ok. Please do tell me if I'm too pushy, hombre. I don't know all the rules, as I only recently stepped into this 'game', you see? Maybe you should explain them to me one

of these days . . . Got a lot to learn still, Señor." *(now please)* "😊 But I can't change the direct way I am. I was born Dutch, remember? Please be clear to me . . . Either yes you want to see me or no you can't because you have to train/clean" *(really ? . . . 😤)*. "I love your texting . . . Keep it coming, sexy 😘"

"Haha, there are no rules, my love" *(my love? something gone missing in translation?)* "I am finished at 20h00/20h30. You can come, but we're not making it long 😊"

"Why? Need your beauty sleep? 😤 Kidding . . . Need me to bring something?"

"Only you 😘"

Mmmmm. Shower!

So there you have it. It is not enough to be direct and tell them what *YOU* want. You also need to tell them to do the same to you. Otherwise, they go all politician on you and leave everything open for interpretation. Glad I got that out of the way . . .

The thing is, he's not my husband, he's not my boyfriend. So I can no longer pretend to be happy when I'm not. And I say/text when I need clarity. Come to think of it—I only called him once, and that was on our first meet.

And *(to come back to the 'age' issue)* what is funny about age, as well, is that everything seems to matter less . . . The couple of kilos too much, my lump, the hemorrhoids, the panda make-up after sex. The noises you make while having sex.

Men our age *don't seem to care*, so why should we?

Up until 2 weeks ago, this was a real issue for me. I sometimes thought, 'Oh hell, what if during sex a man touches your arse and feels your 'friends'? What if he caresses your inner leg and he feels your *(now small again)* lumps? What if he pulls up your legs, and your stomach folds? It's ugly, right?'

I believe that after having lived a monogamous relation for so long, I felt a little insecure for what people would call 'imperfections'. That my body, although *I* am comfortable with it, may no longer please anyone else, as I'm an old bag and a rag doll at that, with all the surgery I had to endure throughout my life.

Wrong, woman! Your presence and enthusiasm will knock him off his socks so bad, he will not care about any of this! He may not even notice . . .

Don't forget, most of the men you meet through dating sites in our age group are either married or have been married before, and they know women's bodies *(probably better than you do)*. Of course, there are exceptions, but in general they prefer having a soft and willing woman instead of an ironing board afraid to mess up her hair. Be eager and your beautiful self. That's all it takes.

To me, wrinkles do no longer exist.

They are now signs of a life well lived.

With ups, downs, and especially a lot of laughter.

-Cassie Date

Which brings me to the learning bit ... you may think you have seen it all and done it all, enjoyable or not, but hey, you'd better wake up 'cause even at age 49, I'm learning. I know NOTHING at all. Up until age 27, I had a very active sex life with lots of different partners. *Yes, this was way before the AIDS issues.* And although I did have one or two elder partners, most of them were my age or slightly older (never younger, though). So yes, I had seen, done, and experienced a lot, but did I learn a lot?

Then I met my 'almost-ex', who was not very experienced, so I taught him what I knew and what I liked. You experiment a little, but always come back to what you both like. And then you become dormant over the space of time. No longer creative. Quick fix. Thinking I had already had it all when I was younger, and should be happy with what I have today. Until I didn't have anything any longer. And for a long, long time thinking I could live with this if on the emotional level we were OK. But that wasn't OK anymore either, and when the emotional reserves finally dried out, nothing was enough any longer. The 'almost-ex' *believes* I have changed *(I definitely have now)*, and I *know* he has changed. Values shift. Communication issues pile up . . . and explode.

Believe me, you *may* love without having sex … loving on a spiritual level. And it *may* go a long way, loving like that. But boy oh boy, having wild sex makes you so much happier! Mind-fucking just doesn't do it for me. I need the physical satisfaction. For mind-*blowing* sex, I will settle.

Well, if you are happy with the way things go in your bedroom, then you are one lucky woman. Because if you are happy in the bedroom, anything else is peanuts and a solution can be found. But, all the women I know complain every now and then. Sometimes often.

Except for my soul sister. But she is so extremely happy with her husband *(after 30 years of marriage!)*, and they were each others' first lovers! Sweet! But she is the only one I know who seems to be fulfilled in every respect.

Ask yourself *(and be honest in your reply)*, 'what am I fantasizing about when having sex with my man? Am I making my shopping list while doing it? Do I make mental notes of things I should not forget? Do I think of the hot waiter who served me my mojito last night?' If that's the case, well, you may want to re-think your situation and start spicing up your sex life.

Even my soul sister, I feel, is prying to find out what happens with Hot Date #1. Does this mean she is eager to learn more about what's going on elsewhere to use it with hubby? I am no prude at all, but for the time being, Hot Date #1 is my business only. Not even my twin sister, with whom I talk about sex much more, knows the details except for whether it is either a marathon or a semi-marathon . . .

Simultaneously to this mornings' text exchange, I was on Messenger with the 'other' Pursuer. The one I am not interested in. He says good morning, and I decide to go all innocent on him. I ask him if he is well. He says yes, and sends me a big kiss. I tell him he is kind and that I feel extraordinarily well—the lake was so beautiful this morning—, and I send him the same picture I sent to Hot Date #1. *See? I am learning. It doesn't have to be a hard job pleasing more men at the same time.* He tells me he would love to walk there with me (*which makes me feel awfully sad because despite meeting once or twice while at the gym, and having supported him while drunk at a funeral, he doesn't know me at all*).

I decide to cool down and show a bit more compassion. I let him know I have no response to that, and that I have already told him more than once I am not a free woman. If he doesn't reply to my message nor shows his intentions, I am not interested in meeting him. He tells me he wants to see me (*he's hot, but also damaged goods, I believe*). I write back I understand, but I am definitely not interested in a fling, and if that would be his intention then I am not in for a meet. *Am I clear now?* But if he wants to discuss and laugh, it would be my pleasure. He wants to spend a good time with a drink and a laugh. So I tell him I like that, with a smiley. He would be pleased. I tell him this week is a bit difficult with the kids off school for 2 days (*and don't forget Hot Date #1*), but I will call him the week after. OK, cool, he is looking forward to that.

I do have to tell you about the above-mentioned funeral because that was rather funny . . . Throughout the service, the Pursuer *(remember, he was extremely drunk)* keeps whispering about who was who at the funeral, and all of a sudden turns to me and whispers, "I wanna make love to you." I bite my lip so as not to laugh out loud or look around to see whether someone else heard. He keeps looking at me, then asks, "Yes?" I tell him to shut up and listen to the service.

Lately, I seem to draw attention from athletic figures . . . Hot Date #1 400m; the Jogger with no idea why he jogs; and the Pursuer, ex-European & world champion & Olympian on both 300 and 400m hurdles. I wonder why . . . Do I carry an Olympic aura because of all the sex marathons?

And I am getting more supple in the process.

There are two kinds of guilt:
the kind that drowns you until you're useless,
and the kind that fires your soul to purpose ...

-Sabaa Tahir

Tuesday, May 3rd 2016
GUILT

Before leaving last night, I had a quick dinner with my daughter. Now, I enjoy that every time 'cause there's never a dull moment with her! My son sits down with us a bit later, as he had been training.

You know what? I do NOT feel guilty about *the affair*. After all, I tried everything to make my marriage work, and the 'almost-ex' has been so clear about not wanting anything to do with me anymore.

But what I *do* feel guilty about is having to lie to my kids about where I am going. I cannot tell them how I feel regarding their father's attitude towards me. I cannot tell them why all of a sudden my mood has changed from desperate to happy.

My kids suffer from our 'adult' situation. How sad that is . . .

And I feel even more guilty because I have been so stuck with myself that I didn't *(want to?)* see it. And didn't do enough to change it. Well, thanks again, Hot Date #1 (and soul sister and twin sister, of course), because you made me realize I was living an endless lie. I had become a zombie, and I needed to seek the fast lane to get the hell out of the situation—unless I wanted to kill my spontaneity for good.

I decide to try and arrange matters as soon as possible so as not to aggravate their feeling of 'not belonging'. But the strange thing is, they are much happier as well. So the saying 'If Mom is happy, everyone is happy' is not *that* wrong.

Upon arriving at Hot Date #1's apartment last night (*mmmm, sweet sweet lips*), he asks me if I missed him. *WTF? Nipples, hang in there.* I thought I misunderstood, I said, 'Excuse me?' And he asks me again if I missed him (*yeah, nipples, go*). Yes, I did. And while he kissed me, my mind

111

started racing. Yes, I really did miss him. I wish I could have met this man at a later stage in my life, though, because he is so freakin' perfect. *Yes, Mom, your voice did come up: If it's too beautiful to be true, it usually is.* No, not really perfect. But handsome, understanding, street-smart, patient, caring, interested, a body to die for, and to me, the best lover *ever.* That's close to perfect, right? Why would he constantly wish to see me? Why does he want to know whether I missed him?

I don't ask the same of him. Am I afraid of an honest answer, or do I simply not care?

No, it is not that I do not care, because I do. At this moment in my life, I just feel I need to enjoy every single day as it comes. I've had enough lemons—I am presently enjoying the tequila and salt to go with it. Maybe a bit selfish? Nah, not at all. After all, this is 'casual dating'. You simply enjoy, knowing one is (still) married and the other is in a relationship of 7 years. Nonetheless, it would be interesting to find out what he feels and thinks about all this. To be continued …

Last night was kind of a sex marathon again, but it now seems to become more and more vigorous. Yesterday morning, the scales were up 200 grams from the eating on Saturday night, but this morning they were down another 600 grams, so minus 800 grams in a week? Voilà, the intensity of making love with Hot Date #1. He loves it when he goes on and on and I start shaking (literally) from the intensity my muscles endure. And still I don't want him to stop.

I guess 'It ain't what you do, it's the way you do it'.

Somewhere in the middle, I told him to fetch oil so I could massage him; then, I firmly kneaded the (*oh my God, so divine*) muscles on his back. He told me I have wonderful hands. (*I know, people tell me all the time, haaa…*) Everything to like about Hot Date #1. Then his buttocks, and his legs. It's definitely all muscle. Hot Chocolate, indeed! But not a sexy massage (*no way, hombre*), only my way to calm him down *(to make you go longer after, Señor!)* But not 10 minutes into the massage, and he ended up on his back with me on top. I asked him to show me what he likes, where to touch him, and how deep. And I have learned.

In fact, I believe that although male penetration is sometimes a topic *(careful with your nails, ladies)*, it is the very suggestion of penetration that is 'hot' to some men.

And in the process, I was pleased by Sex-god's oh-so-intense pleasure mood. Thank you, Hot Date #1. Did *I* please?

After last week's talk about the 'falling in love' red flag, and my message that he should be clear with me this afternoon, the 'tension' seems to have gone, and we talk a lot. About everything. But not *the affair*. Of course not.

I have a coffee and a cigarette. He just smokes. We discuss some more. He has two days off this week, and will be out of town for a long weekend (with his girlfriend). However, could we meet before he leaves on Thursday? I say yes. I have a meeting out of town, but I could come and see him afterwards. He says that would be really nice, and since he doesn't need to wake up for work in the morning, we could make it longer. Time to go before I sexually harass the Cuban Adonis . . . again.

> "Nice dreams 😊, see you soon 😚"
>
> "Sweet dreams, definitely! 😙"
>
> "😊 😚"

Half an hour later:

> "Home safe 😊"

Early this morning, I send him a picture of a wild swan with a "Buenos días, hombre—sleep well? " 😙

> "Ciao, Bella, slept well, need to sleep some more today though 😌 😘" *(et voilà, he does get tired, the Cuban Sex-god)*

> "Mmmm, I had trouble getting up this morning, got up at 07h00 . . . Enjoy your day 😙"

Then, nothing all day. No messages. Nada. So with our new liberated-of-all-constraints arrangement, I decide to write first.

> "You ok, hombre?"

> "Ciao, Bella, all ok, had a tough day, will start my training, will feel better after 😊 And you? All ok? 😘"

> "Mmmm, sorry to hear you had a rough day . . . I am tired but feel satisfied—didn't shower this morning" *(to keep your smell a bit longer)* "😊 Will have a long hot bath after dinner, and an early night it will be for me 😇"

> "That's good 😊 😘"

> "Have a good training—c.u. tomorrow 😊 Want me to bring dinner?"

> "Do we have time to eat? 😌"

> "Dunno . . . I'll bring fruit at least then—shouldn't starve me."

Later that night:

> "Sleep well, hasta mañana 😘"

*Looking like a million dollars is the best statement
for the fool who ceased to see you ...*

Wednesday, May 4th 2016
DROPPING A BOMB

"Already slept 😊 c.u. later, handsome 😙"

"Buenos días, Bella," (@ 6h30) "had to start early. Have a beautiful day 😙"

"😙"

"Bon appétit, enjoy the sun 😙"

"I wish . . . Had dentist this morning & 3 meetings this pm 😊 enjoy your afternoon 😙"

"DaVinci Code, Illuminati & Inferno 😊 the names of the movies I couldn't remember Monday evening—you distract me, Señor . . . "

Then, I send him a text (from Eric-Emmanuel Schmidt) that I found oh-so-appropriate to *all* of our lives . . .

Man is made of choices and circumstances

No one has influence on the circumstances

but everyone has influence on his choices

Later that afternoon:

"Hi, Bella, will you be sad if we push our hot date to next week? " *(WTF, it's only Wednesday—do I have to wait till next week?)* "Can you survive? Would like to go party with colleagues 😣 I am sorry 😙"

I am in a traffic jam on my way to the last meeting.

So that's it? After 2 weeks of exciting dates and great sex, he's standing me up? He's sorry for what? Wanting to go partying? Hell, he's cancelling? On *me*?

Only a minute ago, I still considered Hot Date #1 a potential 'friend with benefits' 'cause I so like spending time with him. Is that what casual is all about? Discard people if you want to do something else? On to the next one? Am I sad? I am *fucking furious! Asshole.* Who does he think he is to cancel on me 3 hours before our meet-up? Too bad I unsubscribed from the site, as I would have had a new date in no time for tonight, only to get the anger out! Fuck him! 'You don't own me' comes to my mind, and I haven't even finished the thought when all of a sudden it is playing through the speakers. Singing out loud . . . But I don't own him either, right? Casual.

And well, yes, I am sad . . . Sad this isn't doing it for me, this online stuff. Sad because I look like a million dollars again *(yes, this time for Hot Date #1)* in my miniskirt and high heels, silk stockings, silk blouse, and the freakin' professional make-up that took me an hour to apply so he could fuck it off in 10 minutes . . . Sad, because I lied to my kids about where I was going these last 2 weeks. Man, this casual scene really sucks! I feel rejected. Well, at least I had fun for 2 weeks. *Was I secretly 'in love' after all?*

"No, not sad. Disappointed, though. Have fun."

"Oh, sorry, my love 😔" *(fuck you too, my love)*

After my last business meeting, I drive back home, and in the car I decide to have more dates. I want to go out and have fun. I am a fast learner. I have to be an 'égoïste' to survive in this parallel world. I was told there were no rules only 2 days ago. But I decide there should be. As in *not ever* cancelling on me. Well, *I* will make up the rules then.

I do not want to know about their reasons why. I do not want to know where they go if they're not with me. They do not get to cook me dinner and tell me about their families. No more feelings. Sex only. Can I do that? Probably not . . .

I also decide this is it. I've had enough. I *am* moving on, and I *will* move out. From now on, it will be my children and my business. Everything else will be secondary. To fit in when it suits me. Not when it suits someone else.

I have dinner with my kids. We sing and dance in the kitchen. *Wild.* How I love them!

Whatsapp conversation thread deleted. Text thread deleted. I feel sad about that as well. It was so sweet. Go online. New profile.

Let's find Hot Date #2 and make up my own terms.

There's only one tiny (read: *huge*) problem . . . I now have such sexy comparison material. Will it be possible to find a similar package?

Yes, Hot Date #1, you woke up the woman in me. And you gave me back the feelings women have, feelings that had blurred out, died, during the second half of my marriage. Rejected and replaceable. Once again. And that hurts. Sweet dreams, indeed . . .

And I feel too much to do this impersonal thing called online dating and *pretend* to feel all sexy just to seduce. Go to sleep. Tomorrow will be another day. And another 300 messages will be there to sift through.

*You can change
what is written in your horoscope.*

*By acting by your highest good,
you can definitely transform
an astrological lemon of a chart
into terrestrial lemonade.*

The sugar is consciousness ...

-Alan Oken

Thursday, May 5th 2016
HOROSCOPE

After a dreamless non-stop sleep of 5 hours, I go out for a walk at 07h05 this morning with my darling dog. Exiting the building, I run into one of my neighbors. She asks whether I want to come over for a coffee after my morning walk. Yeah, sure! I'll get the croissants on my way back.

And you know what? I feel great! The sun is already shining. Still cold. But BEAUTIFUL! And I feel reborn. Why? How come I felt so rejected and used last night, and this morning I feel all sassy and happy? Only because of the sun? I must say I have always been extremely sensitive to a sunny environment. *Hence, Cuban Lover Boy, Hot Date #1?*

Another encounter with the athletically-built jogger, who is more forthcoming than usual with a "Bonjour, madame." Mmmm . . . Would he be Hot Date #2? I say good morning back, and walk on. I'm not interested in luring him out to talk this morning. I want to be alone.

And I start thinking about how I definitely can't imagine having to go through the process of getting to be myself again with a new Hot Date. Being all nervous again on a first face-to-face, having to go through the whole history of self again, having to listen to new Hot Date's life story. I cannot be bothered. *Why can I not just fuck for fuck's sake?*

Because. I am not made that way. I cannot do *it* without feeling attracted to someone. Still, I re-subscribed online last night . . .

As to Hot Date #1, I decide that I will not hold a grudge, because, hey, it's not his fault that I cannot do this casual stuff without feelings. I send him a beautiful sunrise on the lake, and wish him a beautiful weekend and a great Thai massage. And above all, rest. With a winking smiley, of course.

"Ciao, Bella. Gracias 😊 I am still in bed. Enjoy the sun. C.u. soon 😗"

"Mmmm, that's a picture …. C.u. Monday? 😗"

"Yes of course 😗"

And there you have it . . . After careful self-analysis *(and being stood up once)*, I have decided I *cannot* be in love with Hot Date #1. But I still do have a thing or two to learn . . . Dangerous. I am aware. As Cuban Lover Boy is very *very* attractive to me sexually. Whether he is attractive to me otherwise, I still don't know. But you only live today, right? Sooner or later, I will have to tell Hot Date #1 he cannot pull last night's stunt again. I have to make arrangements to see him. I am *not* alone. He is. Well, in a way.

I have mentioned before that I am sometimes philosophical. Sometimes spiritual. And sometimes I look at horoscopes. I know . . . Now *why* did I not think of looking at that before? In the past, I resorted to horoscopes and personality traits when analysing candidates. Why did I not use it to see what would be compatible with me? Apparently, the sex is explosive between Scorpio & Capricorn. So no surprise there . . .

Guess Hot Date #1 is going to stay for another while. Maybe . . .

He has got to learn about compassion, though, as he's now playing with a she-devil. It's written on my forehead, for God's sake. Thinking about getting it tattooed on my inner leg as well.

Guess I am not the only one who can still learn a thing or two. He will also have to.

And I just *know* that I am playing with fire . . .

Nature repeats herself more than one would imagine.
The sea has infinitely more variety ...

-Agatha Christie

Friday, May 6th 2016
HOT DATE #2?

I went online last night, and there's a lot of rubbish to go through. The middle-aged man who wants to meet me straight away because he is sooooo attracted to me *(Remember . . . there are no pictures and no possibility to describe yourself other than with pre-defined fields)*, to again a youngster of 24 whom I tell I have a son about his age and that he should go out and have fun, to which he replies it is too bad I feel that way! I won't bore you with the all the details right now. I am excited about potential Hot Date #2. Here's how it goes:

I see a picture of a body to die for, with a face that looks slightly 'dangerous' *(as in dangerously 'dirty' handsome)*. His name is Mac . . . *Really?* And he's a year younger than I am. He's heterosexual, not tall (1m77), green-brown eyes, short black hair (yes, he does have hair). What he likes about himself are his smile, his stomach *(yeah, I do too)*, and his 'psssst'!

I decide with a body like that I'd wish to feel good on any given day, and at the same time lift up my ego after having been stood up. (Still don't know for sure whether Hot Date #1 saw someone else, but I guess I'm not THAT naïve, right?). Besides, is there talk of 'cheating' if you meet on a casual dating site? Clearly, it means that I was not enough *(or on the contrary, maybe too much?)* for Hot Date #1. And let's face it, if you feel he may be a potential 'friend with benefits', you start developing feelings that can be hurt. And I felt cheated on . . . So let's talk to Mac, who wants to see my pictures . . .

"Breakfast? PS What is the 'pssst' that you like about yourself?"

"Breakfast at Tiffany's 😌" *(a literary Hot Date, nice!)* " My Phallus!"

"Nice one! You inviting me? Ok, what's nice about it ?"

"Of course 😌"

"You make me smile 😊 That's a good start. What are you up to in town, Mac?"

"Drinking a Tequila Sunrise 😌" *(hahaha, really?)*

"You wish! 😗"

"And sex from dusk till dawn! 😌"

"That would be nice 😌"

"Very nice . . . and very hot 😌"

"So what about Phallus (with capital P as you wrote)? What makes him nice?"

"He's gorgeous!"

"Must be with a friend like you."

"And he can make you very happy! A must have! 😌"

"What about you? What are you looking for?"

"Hot sex! With a hot woman!"

"That's clear at least—you're from here?"

"Yes . . . and you?"

"Nope, but never had a local THAT direct 😊 I like that."

"Where are you from?"

"Dutch, lived here half of my life. Besides having sex with a hot woman and drinking tequilas in town, what else do you do?"

"Enjoy my life. Sport. Reading."

"Best one heard tonight 😊 . Yes, that's clear (the sport, I mean.) What do you read? Don't say FT."

"The best is yet to come! ☺"

"Get on with it"

"FT?"

"Financial Times"

"I'm not a banker ☺"

"The best is yet to come? Old Blue Eyes? Banker? Been there done that ☺"

"Sinatra"

"Nice one, Mac. What do you fantasize about?"

"Best actor ever! King of cool!"

"You fantasize about Swoonatra? Hahahaha. I agree, I adore Sinatra. You dance, Mac?"

"Wanna dance, Tequila?"

"Si . . ."

"Tango?"

"It's been a long long time. Start me off slow ☺ Under my skin? "

"Sure. Show me your skin . . . "

"Soon . . . E-mail?"

"Sooner or later"

"Probably ☺"

".....@..... We'll see ☺"

I sent him 2 pictures *(the same I sent to Hot Date #1, as they seemed to work)* . . .

"Love to ☺ Sent"

"Very nice. Thank you, my dear"

125

"Thank you"

"You're a hottie! 😊" *(Haaaa . . . that does an old woman's ego good, Mac . . . go for it!)*

"Thank you, sir. That pleases me"

"Beautiful lips"

"Mmmm ... and they love to kiss. Are you a good kisser?"

"Oh yeah! I love to kiss . . . "

"Good . . . "

"Wanna feel your tongue. On my skin . . . And in my mouth."

"C'est réciproque" *('it's mutual', but in French much nicer, right?)*

"Mais oui . . ."

"Meet? You may charm me some more 😊"

"Maybe. Sooner or later . . .

"What do I read out of that, Mac? We're not 25 anymore, and I'm a big girl. Be straight 😊"

"Maybe we meet sometime . . . "

"All right. I'm off for my beauty sleep." *(after all it's 0h.30)*
"You got my e-mail address . . . Talk soon, sir 😊"

"Sleep well, my dear. Kiss you good night"

"Thank you <3 Wild dreams to you 😊"

"Thank you <3 Wet dreams to you 😊"

"Talk soon 😊"

"Bodytalk! 😊"

But I didn't receive the last message, as I logged off right after the 'talk soon'. So this morning, I reply,

"Mmmmm . . . don't play games, Mac, if you don't intend to
finish them. Had sweet dreams, you?"

And that is (so far) Potential Hot Date #2. Reading back on the
conversation, I feel I may get the hang of this 'casual dating' stuff.
Insinuate, seduce, and arrange a sex date . . . That's all there's to it.
But I have a nagging feeling about Mac. Is he really the single person
he claims to be? Or is he just after online/phone sex? That certainly
doesn't do it for me!

Happy? No. Feel wanted and desired? Yes, still feel good about myself.
And Mac is definitely hot, at least his pictures are. Let's wait and see . . .

Memories of when I was 18 and of mating rituals suddenly pop up in
my mind. Those were the days! Will it be as good now, though? I have
my doubts. Have to get back in touch with my 'predator' buddy from
back then. She'd appreciate my stories . . .

In the meantime, I have proposals from my seemingly-kindred-lost-
soul M.

M is a man I cut off when meeting Hot Date #1, because although I
liked the way he wrote to me, upon seeing his pictures I couldn't
imagine sleeping with him. I believe he was truly hurt by the fact I
didn't reply once he had sent his pictures. He'd better get 'real' straight
away, as casual dating is indeed a jungle. With or without me in it. I'm
sure that in a way he'd felt a bond beyond sex, and maybe I misled
him. The fact is, his pictures didn't attract me. He's just over 50, but
he looks old. A 'Dad' figure. No can do, M. So sorry. I do not reply to
M, as I do not wish to hurt his feelings again.

Another proposal from 'Stud', which brings laughter and curiosity.
Thick and 19-cm long. Hmmm . . . What is it with men, with their
'Pssst', and their need to brag about tooling? Funny and well-equipped
. . . still not enough.

And another one from Maverick, age 47, who's in a town close by every Friday evening and is looking for distraction. Maybe later. He's not tall and not that handsome . . .

There's a picture of another 'hot' body, age 50, no face. I ask for his picture and breakfast, but as he's married, he probably won't get back to me till after the weekend.

And then there's Diego, who is 25, and I start to be curious. He's not handsome, either, but I want to know why he approaches me, age 49. What do all these young men want from me? Accepting their approaches is not healthy in my book! Diego is no longer on line, but I write him I would like to know what he expects from a woman my age.

The Don is 33, and asks me what I am looking for . . . Finally someone asking *me* what I want. I tell him straight out I am doing research for a book. About women around 50 who are looking for their new identity, the search to 'feel and be' a woman again. Women are beautiful and attractive in their own way, but feel insecure as to a 'second' life after 20+ years of marriage. I tell him I am not looking for a 'permanent job', and ask him if he would like to be part of the research. He asks me if I like sex and if I want it now. *Bit silly, Don, 'cause I do not do online or phone sex—at least those boxes are not ticked in my profile!* I tell him I always want sex, but now is not the right time. Send me a picture, Don, and I'll get back to you soon.

Ah, yes, almost forgot about the 'Straight Shooter', codename Lucky Luke. LL is so eager that he forgets to answer my questions, and just wants to see my breasts. I tell him they are too big for a picture. He finds this 'hot', and offers to send an image of his penis. I am not interested in a screenshot of his penis. He's so bloody proud of it that I am immediately turned off. Is a penis a man's best friend? Have to ask next Hot Date. His eagerness sours the exchange. He lets me know that he has literally blasted his screen. At least that is what he said . . . I just wanna vomit.

I later engaged in a conversation with yet another Potential Hot Date—but nothing like #1 and #2 . . .

Codename Bad, 7 years younger, married, tall, 1m94. *I just love tall men.* Green-grey eyes. He likes his hands, his smile, and his 'pssst' . . . *Decide not to ask about that one anymore. Found out that if a man writes this, I prefer to enjoy the anticipation.*

> "Hi, Tequila, I wanna see your picture . . . "
>
> "What are you looking for, Bad? I am curious too—show me yours . . . "

He releases his pictures through the site. He looks all business. Not pretty, no, but handsome and in control. Christian Grey style *(at least the way I pictured Grey after reading the book, definitely not Jamie Dornan in the movie)*. I like it.

> "I am looking for fun and variety. 😊 And you?"
>
> "You seem to be fun 😊 I like to go out, flirt, dance . . . but few possibilities in this country. Do you have an e-mail address for me to send you my picture? Maybe go for a drink somewhere next week?"

I learn fast. No picture on the website. 'Cause even if they're blurred, people will still recognize you, right? M, to whom I had already sent my pictures, would have definitely recognized them if posted.

> "....@.... My hobbies are flying, boats, and basketball. Next week, when?"
>
> "Sent you one from a party 3 years back and a more recent one (bit dopey, but hey . . . you get the picture 😊). Not on Monday/Tuesday, rest of the week flexible. What about

halfway?" (I propose a town)

"Cool, next week not good. How about the following week?"

"Sure. You have my e-mail. Just let me know with sufficient time in advance 😊"

"Noted. The town you propose is good!"

"Grand!"

End of the conversation. Now, what should I do to keep the attraction high? Message him every now and then? Or should I just let him get back to me? Aaaargh. Mac, I can handle. He's very clear. Teasingly so, but clear. Bad, on the other hand . . . I want to meet him, but no clue as to how he wants things done. Let's wait and see.

Facts. There's a diversity of men on the prowl in this alternate world. But some are also looking for something else *(remember M)*. I am definitely still pleasing (my pictures, at least) to men of *my* taste. They even ask me whether the photos are recent. *Do I look younger than 49?* I didn't realize this when I began. Over the years, I have become 'accepting'. Now that I know, I no longer wish to just accept. I decide I will be selective with whom I communicate. They must be tall, attractive, and have a good body *(heavenly, otherwise no competition with Hot Date #1, right?)* Were they to lack the heavenly body, I will need some convincing as to why I would want to meet them. Or else, I should feel there is something worthy of my interest. *No, I am not talking about penis size.*

I feel good! This was clearly the purpose of my exploit. Not to mention an innermost need to be reminded that I am still attractive, that I am still desired. To feel like a woman again, and not just a mom. Even if only in a casual way. I must say the online dating project is quite a success when it comes to that. No more feelings. Harsh, yes. But I need to protect myself. I'm on a new mission. One Hot Date will simply not do any more for the experience. My innermost need having been fullfilled, I am now searching for the reason why I am still desired. Can I do this without 'feeling'? Probably not.

It's a jungle out there. And I'm on the loose . . .

East, 41, a physician, looks really good. In a boyish kind of way. He asks for my picture, I ask for breakfast, and while I'm offline he asks me where. I just reply: "Surprise me." Off to bed. Maybe East replies tomorrow? Love-doctor. Nice.

God, this is a full-time job . . .

One single gift, acknowledged in gratefulness,
has the power to dissolve the ties of our alienation ...

-David Steindl-Rast

Saturday, May 7th 2016

I MISS HOT DATE #1's TEXTING

Yes, I do. I miss his texting. It made me feel so wanted again, and instead I am now chasing around Casual Jungle … It may amuse you guys, but this wears me out. Are there any rules to it? Or do you just go with your intuition?

Still, I can't help feeling rejected, and to be honest, a little angry as well. I have been on such a 'high' for the last 2.5 weeks that I cannot imagine myself ever going back to my loveless sad self. And yet, Hot Date #1 being away for a long weekend now, with no texting whatsoever, makes me miss the connection.

All that added to his having stood me up, and my suspicion that he is back on the site cruising *(me, newly resubscribed as Tequila, whom, of course he did not know)* . . .

Was I unwittingly starting to depend on his expressions of desire for my highs? Because although he said there were no rules, I believe there is one. No texting when he's with the girlfriend, and no texting when he's with the kids.

I conclude that I am most definitely *not* in love with Hot Date #1. You may think that I am in denial because I say this often. However, I feel it differently.

Imagine having lost all *(well, most of)* your sense of womanhood, and someone comes along and makes you feel 'alive' again. Gives you back your feeling of attractiveness, femaleness, sexiness. Basically everything you already had but forgot about. And you desperately need it to recover your self-confidence and feel successful again in your own world. *What would your sentiment be?*

I am eternally grateful for this sexy man to have come into my life. I know it's not going to last forever, and I accept that. Yes, I may be slightly pissed-off for having been stood up; and yes, I may be sad that he may never be the friend with benefits I so want in my life right now, but he still feels good to me.

In short, it's like being immensely grateful to a doctor who's cured you from one ailment or another.

And no, I will not accept just anything to keep him in my life.

I can cope with a wife/girlfriend. Because she's the reason I'm where I am now. And maybe I *could* cope with another mistress *(but I decide I do not want to)* . . . The idea is certainly not pleasing to me. Why? What's the difference between one 'girlfriend' and 'another'? I will have to change my attitude towards all this. No feelings. No hurt. Casual. Right. The word says it all. No questions asked. Sex only. Hot sex. Preferably with a hot Cuban.

I'm lost.

What does all this make me, other than a mistress . . . How would his girlfriend cope? *(If she knew, that is.)* Me, a mistress? I am *fucking awesome!* Heads turn when I walk anywhere on this planet. At least that is what I have been made aware of in the last couple of weeks. Before that, I don't actually know. Hot Date #1 kept texting for more dates. Am I too much for him? Is *he* the one falling in love? With me?

But still, I miss his texting . . .

I start to believe casual dating is good only if you are in a relationship and you want something (or someone) on the side. You say 'goodbye' after your 'make-me-happy fuck', and return to your 'normal' relationship. Much more satisfied and high after some sexual exercising, and thus more committed to your boyfriend/husband.

134

Please note this is NOT who I am, and, in my opinion it would certainly make a poor excuse for cheating. Casual dating is definitely *not* good if you want more than just a 'fling'.

This morning, I get a sweet message from Dude, 58, who is 'engaged', whatever that means. Brown hair, brown eyes, trained body, and above-average equipment. He makes me smile and sad at the same time. So many men out there looking . . . for what?

Here's how that one goes:

> "It's time to think about oneself!
>
> Hello, Tequila,
>
> I asked myself why you advertise here. It is plainly impossible to read a lot on this casual dating profile, and I don't know why, but your profile makes me curious *(yeah, like any other profile you've seen and written to)*. So, nothing else to do but tell you about myself. After a successful career in top management with an international company, I am now an independent consultant and would like to meet an interesting and friendly *(really?)* woman who wants to have more than 'bread and butter'. My body is lean and trained, and am equipped above average *(pleassse, really? who cares.)* I am a bit of a macho *(now, i am beginning to like it!)* Because I am independent, I am flexible time-wise, even during working hours *(whoa, does he do house calls as well, or is he looking for a cheap B&B?)* I've seen on your profile that you enjoy the same things I do *(yeah, sure, hot sex)*. But as I say, I do not know what you are looking for. A man for life *(what part of casual didn't he get?)*, friendship, or only for some quiet hours? *(and quiet they won't be …)*. Are you interested in telling me more? I look forward to your message. Love, Dude. PS I am not curious but would still like to know *(smile)* where you got your nickname Tequila."

135

Ok, that's it! I am pleasantly surprised at the time he took to write me all this. Nice and considerate, so I write back,

> "Hi, Dude! Hope you are well.
>
> At present, only interested in having fun with maybe a ++? Depending on the person I may meet. 😊 Today, still in a complicated marriage situation. But not for long. I have no interest in a 'permanent engagement' at this time of my life, but would like to meet someone once or twice a week. I am not a person to go out and meet different men every week *(yeah right, if a Hot Date is interesting enough, it may be every 3 weeks)*. I prefer spending my energy on my projects, kids, and whatever makes me happy. Nickname: I will tell you one day 😊 But not today 😊
>
> Enjoy the beautiful weather this weekend, and I hope to see your picture when I get back online 😊"

And I decide that the name Tequila suits me. Not sure why. But I like it. Tequila it is.

Let's first penetrate Mac's brain . . . Time for Hot Date #2. Mac is never online till late, though.

Off for a shower and the weekend shopping . . .

*Sex is the consolation you have
when you can't have love*

-Gabriel García Márquez

Sunday, May 8th 2016
MOTHER'S DAY . . .

Yeah, I know—people always do things they like doing *on Sundays* . . .
Why on Sunday? Why not on Tuesday or Wednesday? With their kids
or with their families? Well, my family isn't truly a 'normal' family
anymore, is it?

The eldest recently moved out. The middle one seems to hang out
more and more with his friends, probably to escape from his home
situation. It hurts me to admit this. There's only my little girl, who
seems to *always* enjoy my company. And it is mutual. It's Mother's Day
today. Funny how I always let my children know how little important
these holidays and celebrations were to me. And yet, today, I
desperately crave for the acknowledgement of those who mean so
much in my life. I feel lucky to have my daughter by my side, but at
the same time my boys' absence tears me apart.

I go online to see what's happened last night while I was having drinks
at my neighbor's house. She separated from her boyfriend two years
ago and has been concentrating all her love on their son, in a way that
to me felt quite wrong, unnatural. To the point that her son doesn't
want to sleep anywhere else than at home. I suggested to her to make
it a rule that he sleeps over at his dad's house every other weekend, or
she won't have a life for herself until he moves out *(if ever)*. She laughs
at my exploits and feels that I am right, and that she should also allow
herself time to find a new life. She tells me about the one date she has
had and the commitment issues that appear already. He's been hurt
before and is afraid. I tell her to let him know that they are no longer
18, and that they shouldn't waste time. Go out, have fun, have sex. No
commitment. What if they are not sexually compatible? You want to
wait a year to find out? One of her friends joins us. Her excessively
frustrating behaviour could perhaps be explained by the fact that she
has not had sex for 4 (!) years. She says that the day she meets someone

138

she likes, she'll demand that he takes a medical examination. Huh? Don't get your hopes too high of ever getting laid again, lady! I try to explain *(from my single friends' experiences)* that it doesn't work like that anymore. If chemistry is there, hit the sack! At least you will know whether you want to continue seeing the person or not. I also tell her that if I were a man with a hard-on and she mentioned the medical, I'd lose my appetite on the spot *(right, guys?)* She also mentions she is more into spiritual love. Right, mind-fucking... is that enough? I will believe it when I experience it. I leave them to it, and offer my neighbor to help her get into the online dating scene. She clearly needs the help. And the sex!

In the meantime, M has pulled out all the stops and has written me a third time. If only he could be more attractive... As much as I truly enjoy the way he caresses my mind with words, that's how far the attraction will ever go. Again, I do not reply. Hahaha... talk about mind-fucking! I should introduce him to my neighbors' friend.

'The Enjoyer' is 52, 1m77, brown eyes, brown/grey hair. His pictures (still blurred out) promise an attractive body. He is 'attached', though, and I wonder what it is that binds a man to a woman. I mean, if you're not married and seek entertainment on a site like this, why not *detach* yourself and go the Full Monty elsewhere? I know I would. I am, actually... So yes, I do not know their stories, but still. Would I want to hear their stories again? Most men are probably looking for one-night sex. Like Mac *(but then again this guy is unable to give anything more than a one night stand, at least in my opinion)*. And then there are also 'the others'. Those with whom I feel more connected, whose stories I would love to hear after all. Even when I still want straightforward hot sex, I guess I have always been too much of a people person.

I do not feel like replying to 'The Enjoyer', so I simply ask him to release his pictures.

Do hookers have less business with the existence of these sites?

There you have it! Are women on these sites considered hookers *(to the men in this parallel world, I mean)* who do *'it'* for free? As *I am sure* that all these women who signed up are looking to find exactly the same thing all these men search for … does that make all these men hookers as well?

But that is not what I am looking for, though, am I? I do not want a steady relationship, but not a fling either. I want a 'friendship with benefits'. Singular. Not Plural.

I put this hooker-thought aside. Why not re-register, make up a 'male' profile, and start looking for women? Only to find out what women want here. What motivates them to be on these sites? After all, I have been told on two occasions that these women are extremely aggressive in their approach. I want to find out . . .

Wow!! Men pay to be on these sites if they want to look at a woman's 'full' profile. They also pay to see who looked at *their* profiles. And they pay to approach women. Meaning all the men who wrote/write to me have paid to do so.

100% free for women, though. Very considerate, husbands won't see it on their credit-card statement . . . *Do women not pay the family bills anymore?*

Anyway, I signed-up under Nick, male, 1m83, 49 years old, brown eyes, short black hair. I like straightforward sex, wild sex, sex toys, soft-bondage, underwear, and I am looking for flirting, adventure, longer-term sexual relations. I decide I do not want to pay to approach. Let's sit back a bit and see if and how aggressive women actually are today, and what exactly they are looking for. Oh, and a big sorry in advance to the women who will write to Nick . . . I *had* to find out what it is that other women want *(besides me, that is)*.

According to last Tuesday's text exchange, I am seeing Hot Date #1 tomorrow night. However, I may have to cancel once again. Another lump. Anal this time. Hell-raising and extremely hurting H. I have never had one this bad. And I didn't even go anal . . .

Lump, anal, and hot sex seem all to be associated with Hot Date #1. Off to the pharmacy. See whether we can get rid of it before tomorrow night. If not, I'll have to make up an excuse for lump #2.

What a woman has to do to have good sex . . .

Hot Date #1 is back from his long weekend with the girlfriend.

> "Hola, Señora, how are you? It was a long weekend." *(Don't I know it. Why was it long for him? Imagine his girlfriend writing the same thing to her lover if she had one. How would he feel about that?)* "Have a nice evening 😊"

I ignore the message and write back 3.5 hours later. After all, *it is still weekend.*

> "Hola, Hombre, I was at a restaurant with my 'horrible 3' 😊
>
> Hope your weekend, even though long, was nice 😌
>
> Sweet dreams 😗"

I realize that the past couple of weeks have been so extraordinary I had the wish to be so much desired like this forever. And *imagined* Hot Date #1 as a potential 'friend with benefits'. Today, I feel I was plain *wrong!*

Different mindset. Look at what *is*, not at what *if*. The 'what is' you have *right now* and you can enjoy it. The 'what if' creates expectations, and you may forget to enjoy the 'what is' today. Oh, I am so complicating things . . .

I check back on the site to see if there's anything 'playing', but guess

Sunday nights are for family and 'attachments', or else everyone is out having sex in the sun this afternoon. All quiet. Only two messages for Tequila and one for Nick. Unless Nick pays for his subscription, he will not be able to get in touch with potential hot dates . . . Let's leave it till tomorrow.

H is killing me, even after getting proper medication from the pharmacist. Sorry, Hot Date #1, I will be travelling late tomorrow. With lump #2 ☺

Sacred signs
always come out
when your soul calls out
in pain or joy …

-*Lawren Le*

Monday, May 9th 2016
PUTTING THINGS ON ICE

Something extraordinary happened during my morning walk. I was talking with the Jogger, whom I now bump into on a regular basis. All of a sudden, from the corner of my eye, I noticed something fly past me, and I hear a thump on the grass. Baby squirrel doesn't hesitate as it smells the danger, and gets up ready to escape. Another dog comes running and jumps right onto him. Oh, I felt *so* bad, I thought that was going to be the end of the cute baby. I start retching. Then *(all this happens in 2 seconds, right?) my* dog, my *hero*, jumps onto the lady's dog and howls. I swear he was crying!

I have tears in my eyes, as this was truly the one thing he could do for the other dog to let go, and for the baby squirrel to get home free.

Now, my dog is one who goes hunting in the woods, and I do not 'walk the dog' when in the forest. *I* walk. And he chases scents. If lucky, I find him sitting by the car when I return. I guess he must have picked up my distress. I was so proud of my dog!

This was surely a sign of some sorts. An omen you don't immediately figure out. Am I the squirrel? And my dog someone who will save me? If someone else is the squirrel, am I the one to save that person? *Probably, my feelings are the squirrel . . . Now where the fuck is the dog that will save them?*

Extremely curious as to how this is going to work out . . . I may have to wait a thousand years for it to happen. But it will. It always does.

Upon getting home, I send one of my morning pictures to Hot Date #1.

"Buenos días, Señor, hope you are well (😊 😊)."

Nothing is wrong. Although I don't understand him, I still like Hot Date #1. I have decided to continue as last week. But my feelings towards this handsome man have definitely changed. Slightly icy, more suspicious. Jealous? No. Disappointed? Yes. By him? No. By my own feelings.

Then I call the hospital to get help with lump #2. OK, I did well with the medication from the pharmacy, but I may want to put things 'on ice'. How do you put your asshole on ice? OK, I will spare you the details, but it's simple. Very uncomfortable, but it works. In the meantime, I must have regained 2 kg, as I have not been able to go to the toilet since Friday. The day starts well with squirrel being saved by my hero, but then it goes from bad to worse.

> "Ciao, Bella, all is ok, a lot of work, and you? Have a nice day 😊 😘"

I write him the squirrel story and say I am puzzled by the 'sign', the 'Omen'.

> "Nice story 😋 Bon appétit. Enjoy your day 😗"

> "I will 😊 U2"

OK, that's it! I will *not* see him tonight. A '*nice story*'? I'm telling him something 'weird' happened, something exceptionally 'special' to me, and I receive a '*nice story*' back? Maybe I should stop doing this altogether with Hot Date #1. Maybe not so considerate after all. But giving up good sex? I'll stay around for the sex, of course, but definitely *not* tonight. *He* can ask for it now.

Hot Date #1 texts me whether I want to come over for 20h30. With a smiley. *Sure I want to come. But not over for 20h30. Forget it.*

How strong is *your* intuition? If my sixth sense finally kicks in and I

145

suspect something *not* based on facts, I am usually right. Not always. But most of the time.

And yes, I am right again. It is indeed Hot Date #1 pursuing Tequila. Why am I not surprised?

I text him back saying that I still have this meeting at 18h15 with the dean of some hotshot school for my project, and that I may run late. I'll call. Or if he prefers seeing me another time this week, that is fine as well. With *two* kissing smileys.

10 minutes later:

> "Ok, tomorrow 20h00? That would be perfect 😊 😘"
>
> "Will try to arrange—talk tomorrow—wish me luck—hotshot school good direction for my project 😊"
>
> "All the best, you'll make it 😘"
>
> "I know, but nervous anyway . . . Gotta go 😘"
>
> "😊 😘"

In the meantime, I see that he's back online chasing Tequila. Finds my (fake) picture sweet. I tell him I like his picture as well. Tequila . . . he prefers drinking Cuba Libre. *Don't I know it* . . . I tell him I like Tequila Sunrise. Sweet and sunny. I ask him what he is looking for and whether he has an easier name than the code the dating site assigned him. No reply.

I think I may have strayed past the casual line. With an unclear situation at home, it was important that everything 'outside' was simple and clear. This is who I am. Open, direct, honest. Which complicates things for most people.

Note to self: next time, be more cunning . . .

146

Oh well, at least he didn't lie. He just didn't communicate he wanted to see other women. And that would have been something I would have liked to hear, and probably even *understood*. I am getting a bit restless . . . I am definitely not going to deal with another mistress. On the other hand, I do enjoy challenges!

"I know" (*Irma, ft. Youssoupha*) is playing in the background . . .

Tequila, anyone?

Throughout this journey of life,
we meet people along the way.
Each one has a purpose in our life.
No one we meet is ever a coincidence …

-Mimi Novic

Tuesday, May 10th 2016
TWIN

And a true lady she is, title and all. My twin sister. Twin from a former life. Gone wild at age 49 . . .

How is it possible that we laugh so much at each others' exploits? Are we truly that funny? Or do we just understand each other so well on a certain level? What is it that makes us so open, as if we've known each other for a lifetime?

She is a writer. You may find her stories about her travels amusing. This was the period when she decided to begin living her youth. Recognize it?

We talk about Hot Date #1 & Schwanz, her latest exploit. *I leave you to it to search the German dictionary for the meaning.* We eat and drink and laugh. A lot. Yet another thing we share: we find humor in practically every situation.

Before she leaves, I ask her advice on the anal issue. She loves anal sex, but it won't get her to climax. Also, make sure your partner is not too big. And, of course, anal sex requires some preparation. A thorough rinse of your 'behind' is definitely advised, as well as proper lube.

Thank you, lady—now let's go back to hospital to get lump #2 out of the way . . .

The comparison of others
leads to disappointment.
The comparison of self
leads to improvement

-Avina Celeste

Wednesday May 11th, 2016
HOT DATE #2

Not going to bore you with the details of the texting this time. I met up with Mac last weekend. Mac is everything his pictures promised. Hot body, only muscle. Soooo strong. And his looks. There is an aura of danger about him. I like the package. His first words, "Oh my, you're even hotter than the pictures you showed." *Yes, Mac, I know. Get on with it!* But, of course, he did score some points with that remark. Drink? Yes, please. He returns with a Tequila Sunrise. *Sunrise at sundown, nice, good move, Mac.* "So, Tequila, what's your real name?" I tell him Tequila it is and will remain. At least for the time being. His touch of danger foretells me to be careful. I already have a 'jogger stalker'. One is enough. "Wanna dance, Tequila?" *Holy shit, what's this? Did he speak with Hot Date #1?* And then I remember we talked about dancing during our first exchange. 'Sure, Mac' (with a touch of disinterest). And we dance . . . Sinatra is singing "Under my skin." More points for Mac, as he's read back our texting. And I feel that I please. Again. A lot. No, this time, really a LOT . . .

Mac is a hot, rather straightforward lover. Not a lot of fantasy when it comes to 'positioning'. *It's an art, right?* On the other hand, there was his 'Psssst!' to please me. So, overall, a satisfying experience. His body was lean and strong. Nipples still reacting to the memory. He also talks dirty during the act. And when I say dirty, I mean *nasty dirty*. Not sure I am into that, though . . . I love it if I excite a man, but to that point? Get a grip, Mac! Don't go nasty on *me!* He wants to meet again. I tell him I'll call him. I'm a fast learner.

I feel restless. Hunted. Or rather haunted?

Hot Date #1 wanted to see me last night. I texted him that I was at the hospital and would let him know when finished. He writes back 'no stress'. Not, "What's up?" Not, "Are you OK?" No. Just 'no stress' . . . I text him at 20h00 to go and have fun, as I'll be at the hospital for a while. His response: *Oooh* 😊 *another time* 😳

Nothing this morning. No texting. I guess I managed to lose Hot Date #1's interest. But at midday, he asks whether I am OK and to enjoy my day.

Tell him I'm OK now, and that I missed his messages in the morning. Did something change? *Would like to see you* 😳

He reassures me that all is fine, and it would be superb to see me on Friday, if that is OK with me. I reply that I have meetings, but will finish early and that, *Oui . . . me réjouis* 😳

It is not fair. Although we accept that people are different, we do compare. And even though I do not want to compare, Hot Date #1 is *too* sexy and hot to *not* be comparison material. And 'nice' sex just isn't *it* anymore. Though it would have been 30 years ago . . . *OMG, that long ago already?*

Later that evening:

> "Ciao, Bella, how was your day? How are you?" *(does he truly care?)* "Enjoy your evening 😊"

> "Hola, Hombre . . . Long day—Friend picked me up from hospital this morning and I had a coffee (and a drink). Too late to make lunch for my kids 😊 Had 2 meetings this PM—tired now . . . You had a nice day, Señor? 😳"

> "Yes, quiet and pleasant, luckily. At home now watching TV. Get well. Looking forward to Friday 😊 😳"

And there it is again . . . He wishes me to get well, but why not ask me straight out what it is that took me to the hospital in the first place? Not that I am comfortable talking about lump #2, but it would have been nice to ask . . . Does he care at all? Is he being discreet? What

152

the fuck do I do with this man who keeps on cruising endlessly . . . I can't stand being put aside without knowing the reason, and I am not the time-sharing type either. Being straight with me, I can handle, and would accept. I still want him. Sooo sexy . . . it's almost criminal.

"I am reading . . . Me too, Hombre 😙 Sweet dreams"

"Gracias, you too 😊😙"

Self-doubt is a persuasive mistress;
careful not to shag her
or you'll never get your balls back ...

-Dannika Dark

Thursday, May 12th 2016
RAINY DAY

Sent a picture to Hot Date #1 of a rubbish bin on which is written 'I want it all'.

> "Hahaha, even the local rubbish bins want it all 😵—feeling motivated 😊 Have a beautiful day 😙"

Aïe, perhaps I chose a wrong picture for him. May send the wrong impression. Too late, though . . . Do hope he picks up on the meetings I had this week that were awesome boosters for me, and the 'feeling motivated' does apply to me and has nothing to do with him . . .

> "Ciao, Buenos Días, yeah looks that way 😊 Gracias, enjoy your day 😙"

In the meantime, lump #2 is not an H but a thrombosis. I'm still sitting on ice and taking anti-inflammatories. Frickin' anal.

After having gone through the 45 messages from a hot Tuesday afternoon during the last two days, I start to feel tired of all this. How do women do it *all the time?* I now have 3 Hot Dates drooling. Well, #2 is. And #3, I don't know till next week. #1 keeps me off-balance. Casual dating is definitely *not* for me. I decide I want to be a 'real' mistress. With perks, of course. I've never been a mistress as of yet. How do I become a mistress? Let's ask my single friends who are currently looking for a cyber-produced soulmate. They will know. They are 8-10 years ahead of me. I feel like a virgin looking for answers. Yeah, right . . . why not?

And now I do have to switch off. Too much analytical 'work'. Stop thinking about heavenly bodies. Get on your way, babe, and work on your projects. That's now your priority.

But first, go buy some books and fix lunch for the kids.

"Lunch break 😊 Bon appétit. Are you ok? 😗"

"Si, Muchacho 😊 y tu?" (*Incorporating some new words,
have to at least try and learn Spanish. Even if it's only all the
different names I can call men. May come in handy some day*
😌)

And at 18h00:

"All well, wish you a nice evening 😘"

"Thanks. German course 😊 Enjoy your evening 😘"

"😘"

"Thank you, looking forward to tomorrow 😘"

When a man takes a mistress,
he doesn't turn around and divorce his wife.

-Arthur Golden

Friday, May 13th 2016
MISTRESS IN THE MAKING

"Buenos días . . . Have a nice day 😌"

"Hola, Chico . . . Get ready . . . Going to be a stormy night 😊"

Want me to bring something?

"Haha, it's ok. I think you know what I need, haha 😌"
(Really, Hot Chocolate? I'm not too sure about my part in this story anymore—I kind of lost control over the situation . . .)

"Noooo . . . Tell me 😇"

"Honey, believe me, you cannot give me what I need 😌"
(WTF? Is he intentionally being an arse or am I reading this wrong? Did I really understand this right?)

"Why should I come then? 😌" *(actually considered jogging pants and sweatshirt, no make-up)*

"Yeah, sure 😊 😌" *(yeah, sure what?)*

"It was a joke . . . You asked me once what I was looking for, and I told you I would like to find a bag full of cash, remember? 😜" *(Ah, yeah, forgot about it . . . but that was when you were still 'really' nice, though . . .)*

Now can someone please stand up and tell me why I always think the worst of a situation? Hahaha . . . why is it that I always seek the best in people, and yet whenever I misunderstand a statement, I always suspect the worst? Should I follow my intuition, or is my intuition misguiding me?

"Sorry, can't help there 😬"

"☺ ☹"

Since yesterday, I have been asking around on 'how to *become* a mistress' and 'how to *be* a mistress'.

First, how to *be* a mistress.

Two of my friends tell me it has been sheer torture. One suffered it for 2 years, the other for 7.

The first spent two years as the mistress of an 'attached' man, not even a married man. A local politician. She informed me that she'd done it because she was in love with the man and was made to believe he was as well. She had been at his beck and call for almost two years when she decided she had to fall out of love with this man who would never give her what he had promised all along. It was hard, to say the least.

The second had been with her lover for 7 years. This man was, in my opinion, stingy as hell. First, they met on a weekly basis just for sex, in a 'hotel' where rooms cost, at the time, €25 for 2 hours. Later, every day at lunchtime, whereby she would drive half an hour just for a snog in his car, then drive half an hour to get back to work. She had a real problem. She was deeply in love with the man, and she accepted a 'make-believe' on his part. However, she managed to convince herself that one day he *would* actually leave his wife. She was in love, frustrated, and (as my first friend) at the man's beck and call. One day, she demanded that he make up his mind, and gave him a 5-year (!) ultimatum. He found that unfair, but neverthless accepted to deliver in only 3 (!) years. In the end, it only took him 2 (!) He chose to stay with his wife. My friend shed more tears over him than when she divorced after 32 years of marriage. She was so depressed that she contemplated suicide. Over the years, she was offered to become a mistress on more than one occasion, but she ended up marrying the love of her life. No. Not the stingy lover-boy. A new man she met shortly after ending the affair.

OK, now that is actually *not* how I imagined being a mistress was all about. Perhaps I glorified the 'position' just a wee bit?

Definition of Mistress:

1. a woman in a position of authority or control.
2. a woman (other than the man's wife) having a sexual relationship with a married man.

I guess in my mind I am making up a new definition by mixing 1 and 2, which suits me much better. I want it all. The rich guy *(although I don't care about money anymore)*, the hide-away apartment, the holiday/business trips, the spoiling. And not only if he wants to see me, but ideally I want to be in the mood as well. Because I will also have my business to tend to, right? Yes, I can imagine myself in *my* definition of a mistress. Just for the experience.

Oh yes, and he would be sooooo crazy about his mistress that he would do anything for Princess Tequila . . .

Fairy tale?

Now, a bit more difficult to answer . . . How to become a mistress, that is find a friend with benefits 'plus' fringe benefits?

According to friend number 2, you just roll into that. If I want it my way *(the total package)*, then I will have to cruise in a more aristocratic environment. She is used to living in high society, so she should know about this. But still. She *was* with a stingy bastard who probably never intended to leave his wife in the first place, and he enjoyed my friend on all levels for seven bloody years! But still, the stingy bastard *was* floating high. She is entertaining, beautiful, and extremely generous. And if I have to take her word for it, a tigress in bed as well. At least I imagine that from the stories she tells. How come he chose his wife over her? *No entiendo.*

160

Cruising in higher circles being one alternative, the other was to be noticed.

That I can do. But then again, I am getting noticed all the time lately, yet that didn't get me anywhere. OK, I admit that I did not give the 'mistress' option a *real* thought until yesterday, but still ... I touched the mistress-subject when talking about Hot Date #1 because in a way I am/feel a mistress *now* on a casual level. *Which leads me of course to wonder if it truly is casual. Don't we see too much of each other for it to be casual?*

So, how to cruise in higher circles? Smoke a joint and hope to get *that* high? I searched on line how to become a mistress, but all I found is a lot of information on how to *behave* once you are a mistress and what to expect once you're found out. I believe I can imagine how to do this. But do I really want to do it?

Oh, man, just stick to the friend with benefits . . . isn't it all the same on one level or another?

I spoke with my soul sister today. She's been reading the initial chapters of my memoirs, and she's over the moon. That definitely got me in a *happy* mood. Because she is like me in a way. When we read and feel attracted to the story, we're drawn into it and manage to actually merge with (thus *become*) the character. So through me she is actually having an affair. Hahaha ... So funny, for this woman is straight as an arrow, as straight as I used to be until a couple of weeks ago. She, on the contrary, would not have any of it! My soul sister tells me not to burn my wings, to which I reply that I found out a long time ago there is 'crush' and there is 'in love'.

'Crush' involves wearing make-up and pretty dresses or torn jeans, whatever your mood may be. You please and let yourself be pleased. Yes, you like the guy, are attracted to him, and you feel good about yourself. Even though you would like to see him more *(because he makes you feel so good)*, you are happy without him as well. BUT . . . you do not wash his socks. That to me is Hot Date #1.

Now 'In Love' . . . that is something else. Someone has triggered you so bad that you can't help making a fool of yourself. You just cannot get enough being around him. You are happy all the time, grin stupidly, and are willing to let him see you even without make-up. You would like to show him everything you've got to give. He is the one for whom you would make dinner every night. The one you trust as much, or more than yourself. The one that makes you feel worried if he doesn't text or call. The one who stirs anticipation for the good vibes you know will be coming. And yes, you'll even wash his socks. Now THAT is what 'In Love' is all about.

And the trick is to keep both separated. I used to be very good at that. But of course, this was a long time ago.

The dating site is put to rest for the time being. I will still check out the messages, but there will be no active 'hunting'. I'm getting tired of this. Definitely will meet Hot Date #3, Bad, next week. If he has the decency to contact me as promised, that is. Just to get a taste of the 'Grey' feeling. How many alpha males can a girl handle in 5 weeks? Have to draw a line somewhere. I feel exhausted.

> "I finish early but wanna see a friend before coming to see you. 19h00-19h30 ok for you? "
>
> "Hi, Bella. That would be great 😊"

I will probably be late … 😈

162

Rigid rules and expectations
lead to disappointment

Saturday, May 14th 2016
HOT DATE #1, Part VI

11 days without sex with Hot Date #1 almost made me forget the intensity of it all (*I did say almost, not entirely*). My feelings during his absence had become a bit 'frigid'. I tried to make him out the big bad wolf. And gee, it *is* casual, right? But the good feeling is back instantly upon seeing him.

Forget about Hot Date #2. He was only a lot of talking, no skills, not interesting. And we already established that I am not sex-only material. Plus the dirty talking … Quite cheap. Too casual for my taste?

I almost feel like I have cheated on Hot Date #1. *WTF is that all about? I do not have to justify anything to anybody. You don't own me, remember? And I don't own you.*

Give me Hot Date #1 with the right mindset and I may even consider being at *his* beck and call for a period of time. I did say 'consider', because however you name it I am not the 'beck and call' type. Not even for sex. Or rather, *not only* for sex. In a way, I *already am* a mistress with him being 'attached' to a long-term relation. *And while we're at it, let's not forget that I am still married.* But I want the Full Monty. While I am rediscovering myself, I want to experience it all! New hunting strategy to sort out.

As I arrive, I am still laughing on the phone with my twin sister. A good thing I did call her, as she tells me she's in love. Where the hell did that come from? Well, she spoke with a Scandinavian on the phone in the morning; he invited her for lunch, and she instantly fell in love with the Viking. And he as well, apparently. I hear that he was flying back to Scandinavia to cut off all ties with a casual relation. *Do those two words go together? Casual and relation?*

I had already decided in the car that I was going to be my all-positive self. And not bring up the 'casual dating site' subject.

There he is, smiling at me. He draws me against him, and then turns to fix us some drinks. So, upon asking how I was (*God, he's just so handsome, so extremely sexy*), my former tribulations vanished into thin air. I didn't *need* to be my all-positive self anymore. I was all happy and gay, and I literally push him up against the wall while kissing. *Wow . . .* Later, I tell him that my week was excellent and I am the world's greatest, as that is how I feel. I give him a small present, sexy Dutch shower gel that foams with water and feels like a gentle caress. Mmmm, so good. He says he didn't know it, and will now think of me also when showering. *Huh? Also? Am I purposely misunderstanding all the time? When else?* I tell him about all the good things that happened this week, and he asks me about hospital. Even though desperate for hot sex, I must tell him about lump #2, right? I am also glad that maybe, just maybe, he felt uncomfortable to ask. Discreet via texting, yet not disinterested?

So I tell him that dealing with stress leaves me quite constipated, and the meeting from last Monday finally did me in. I tell him how I'd been packed 'on ice' in hospital, and my presentation of the facts draws a laugh out of him. I say a normal person would have H, while *I* get to deal with anal thrombosis, in the same way a normal person would have 'a spot' when nervous while I get to have reverse acne. *Really Hot Date #1, nothing is normal about me, so if you want to run, this is the time!*

Who knows, maybe I'm getting the hang of it: no complaints, turn a negative experience into a funny adventure, and the world is at your feet! So was Hot Date #1 at that moment.

"Obviously, this means I cannot touch your arse when making love to you."

"Yes." (*Yes, Señor, you got that right. Not that it hurts anymore, but I would feel so uncomfortable, you feeling lump #2.*)

He's made dinner, and asks me if I'm hungry. I tell him I'm hungry for sex. He laughs. *Get on with it, Hot Date #1, before I take the initiative and tackle you!* He fixes us a Cuba Libre. We talk about everything and nothing. Is this the 'getting to know each other even better' part? I don't actually care *(point to self, not caring)*. I'm on a 'high' and he's amused by my stories. He tells me about his week, and that he left work early that afternoon to have a siesta and cook for me. Nice one, Hot Date #1. He just keeps scoring, this Sex- god, doesn't he? *Think of Tequila, think of Tequila . . .*

He then leads me into the living room 'cause he wants to do something with me. *Oooohhh, finally.* He puts on music and says, "Now it's time you learn Cuban salsa. I want to take you out, but you have to be able to dance with me." *Now THAT would be hot, wouldn't it? 'Meet the Querida' vis-a-vis his dancing mates? And a whole space full of hot Cubans at the same time? Won't happen! And why does he want to take me out?* He tells me I'm a fast learner *(if only you knew how fast, hon)*. And I think to myself how hard it is to dance when you're high with desire and every touch sends electricity through your body, not to mention the clear signs that he is also in need. I let him know it is hard for me to be led, as I have only recently regained my independent personality, and so I must be the one in charge.

He whispers to let go. I close my eyes and concentrate on feeling his hands, listening to his voice as he leads me. My mind is now empty. I let myself be led . . . He decides *(yes, I told you he's a macho)* that was enough for today. When I turn around, he's almost naked. *OK, may I attack now? I am hungry for some hot Cuban dancing in bed.*

I make it an issue to dress for Hot Date #1 every time I go see him, and he clearly appreciates it. Showing up in torn jeans, he tells me I look like a teenager; but wearing a dress and heels, I look really good, nice, sexy. Today, a Burberry mini-skirt, black silk stockings *(with frivolous and hot details he doesn't seem to care about)*, an oversized linen sweater *(you have to wear something in between sex-rounds to avoid sitting naked in the kitchen, right?)*, slightly see-through to show a hot blood-red bra *(that he doesn't seem to care about, either)*, and high heels to die for. With stockings, I do not do panties, ever. Never did. Sex on legs, indeed.

Which reminds me of a wedding story. A friend of my almost-ex' was getting married, and we attended the reception with our daughter, who was all excited, as it was her first time at a wedding. She was about 3-4 years old. During the reception, I went to the toilet with my little princess, and while squatting, she asked why I was not wearing any underwear. I explained that if you wear a skin-tight cocktail dress, the visible lines of underwear will ruin the effect. Not a pretty sight. Better learn young. We washed our hands and walked back to the castle gardens towards my almost-ex, who was talking with some men. My daughter ran up to him with a secret smile on her angel-face and cried, "Daddy, daddy . . . mummy doesn't have any knickers on!" Everything went still all around. Quite embarassing. Head up high, smiling self-assuredly and maybe a bit arrogantly, I walked towards my almost-ex while people stared at me. I could *feel* them thinking . . . Yet another lesson for my little one: whatever the circumstances, always remain dignified!

The shoes were gone before the dancing, as they were only made for walking. The stockings went carefully and slowly under a 'hmmmm'. Skirt up and sweater up, but definitely not off. And that was how Round #1 started. *How come I, at age 49, can excite someone so much? Especially a man I believe could have anyone he wanted. Oh yes, I remember . . . I am fucking awesome!*

Man, this is becoming an addiction that will be quite hard to kick . . .

After Round #1 *(about two and a half hours later, thus a half-marathon for me)*, I put on my oversized sweater and ask for socks. He looks at me as if to ask 'why?', and I explain we have some more dancing to do.

Surprised face. For real? Yes, for real. *I will be less distracted now that I have had sex.*

But first, we have another drink, dried meat, and some chocolate I brought. We talk more. About old boyfriends and girlfriends. About discussions we have with our friends. About our kids. I tell him we have to set a 'fixed' day so the lying to my kids can be made easier. I'll just tell them I'll go to yoga (*aaargh*). He asks what day is good, but we leave it at that. He then tells me he has to do his duty, text his girlfriend. *Hang on there, cliffhanger . . . Is it a duty for him to text me, as well?* And I ask him if he ever feels guilty towards his girlfriend. He doesn't answer and changes the conversation. So I ask him why he doesn't reply, as I want to know. Because *I* do not have any guilt feelings. Even though still married, I do not have a relation anymore. And I am curious. Not jealous. Can a person do this without a guilt-trip? I don't think I could. I already feel a pang of guilt having had sex with Hot Date #2 while still doing it with Hot Date #1 . . . WTF, right?

I wonder why the rules I came up with some days ago do not apply to Hot Date #1. Is it because he was already there before the rules were drawn? Or is it that I lack the information I am after? Do I really want to know all the answers?

I tell him that if a woman is in love, she wants more. She wants to live with her man and/or get married to him, and wants him to be with her *all the time*. Although he speaks very highly of her, I feel that he is hesitant to commit to her. *Is it only because of the sex issue? Or is there more to it?* He doesn't say. But yes, he does feel guilty sometimes, but, no matter how much he has tried to change the situation, she just cannot deal with his needs. *That's OK, hombre. No worries, I'll deal with them.* He adds that the same thing happened with his ex-wife. Everything went well at first, but she later lost interest. *So he's in a dilemma. Either accept the way things are with your girlfriend, get over it and move in with her, or find yourself what you need and again face the risk of it going sour. There is always a third alternative: to continue as is.* I tell him not to despair, that the answer would come when he needed it. But secretly, I wish for him to choose the third alternative. I ask him if she knows. He looks at me, questioning. I ask whether his girlfriend knows about his affairs . . . He tells me that she does. But he's joking. Thank God. Otherwise, *I* would have been on a guilt trip . . . And that is clearly not *my* issue to deal with.

It gets me thinking, though. I can understand his ex-wife. Of course you are always interested in intimacy with your husband. But having kids, a full-time job, a household to run . . . If you do not take time to be together, sex is definitely the first thing to downgrade in your relation. Is that where we women go wrong? No longer making time to be physical with our hubby?

But what about them? Our men? Don't they have to do the same? What if they came home one Friday evening, after previously having packed our stuff and arranged for someone to babysit during the weekend, and they told us, 'Come on, babe, let's hit the road together', and we ended up in a hotel for some serious love-making, without leaving the room for 2 days straight?

He also tells me he had once tried meeting someone through a site. *Sure, only once? Yeah, right!* And that it was a flop. He had also had a one-night stand with someone he met while out dancing. He had been clear about his situation and didn't want anything else but the one-nighter. She, on the other hand, wanted more and started clinging in need before his dancing buddies. Some things never mix. *Then why does he want to take me dancing?*

And then *(Why the hell would I bring this up now?)* I blurt out that I want to be a mistress. Just for the fun of having lived it. As long as I am not ready for a steady, I may as well experiment what's convenient for me and what is not. I tell him about my friends who have been mistresses, how difficult it was for them, and that I see it completely different. What does he think of that? He says I would have to ditch him first . . .

169

Mmm, wait and see, hombre . . .

We talk more about work, our individual projects, and he tells me the secret to having it *all* is 'patience'. I am definitely not the patient type of girl. If I want something, I make damn sure I get it. Unless it involves the emotional kind of wanting. Then, I am rather timid.

I get up and say I am in need of some more teaching. *After all, he did give me socks.* He takes my hands and leads me towards his living room. But if I remember well, we didn't make it through the hallway, and somehow I ended up in his bed in no-time. That's the price to pay if you want to dance naked with only a shine-through sweater on. And man-socks. Sexy . . .

Time and space are blurred, and I am disoriented as to where I find myself on the bed whenever I am with this extremely mind-disturbing man. No need for blindfolds. Somewhere halfway into a sexual struggle, snuggled up, I tell him he is beautiful. And ask about marks on his body. I want to know whether his penis has a name. He laughs and says that his penis doesn't have one. *It should, however.* I ask him what he wants. "You," he says. *Well . . . here I am. For now.* He asks me what I want. I reply that I want something I can't have right now. I don't look at him but I can feel him looking at me in a state of surprise. I tell him I want anal sex. He asks me to repeat, as he didn't understand (*but I think he did*). I repeat. No-name penis immediately stands at attention. And the heat is on. Again. Of course no anal, for obviously lump #2 is still there (*which is why I could bring up the subject, right?*) Maybe another time, Hot Date #1. I got what I wanted, merely by being my canny self. Happy? Yes, actually I am. And soooo fulfilled. I want more of this. Now. Hot Date #1 mumbles that next time he'll have to tie me up so I stop avoiding climaxing. Hell, how many orgasms can a girl handle in one evening?

"Sweet dreams 😊 😴 😴"

"😊"

I switch on my music and "One Night Stand" by Janis Joplin comes on. I do not believe in coincidences.

"Home . . . Sleep . . . 😴"

By the way, we didn't have dinner.

"Buenos Días, mi amante 😊 Today I feel 'taller than tall'.
Thank you for making me feel so good. Enjoy your girls 😊"

"Buenos días, Bella, slept till now 😊 Gracias, enjoy your day too 😴 🐾"

It is now early evening, and I should be making dinner, but I am not hungry, nor is my daughter. And the boys are not here. Neither is the almost-ex. So no dinner. I'll have an apple instead. I take my darling dog for a walk. As we turn the corner to walk by the riverside, I catch a glimpse of a boxer ... Boxing into empty space. (*Mmm nice, another athlete; where the hell have they all been while I was so unhappy?*) The man seems to be extremely concentrated. We do not get to see this every day. As a matter of fact, I have never seen this man here before, and I do come here often. The dog found it strange as well, and starts growling. The boxer turns around, looks truly afraid, and says: "Oh my God, I thought I was about to have a heart attack." To which I reply, "Scared?" "Hell, yeah!" is his answer. I ask him whether it was the dog or me who got him scared. He gives me a dead- serious look: "Madame, you couldn't scare me even if it were after dark and you were a vampire." *Thank you, Boxer, I'll take that as a compliment . . .*

All quiet on the online dating front. I guess everything comes in waves. Haaaa!

I have developed extremely contradictory feelings. Up until getting to Hot Date #1's apartment, I was convinced he was definitely looking for another lover (in addition *or* replacement). Now I am not so sure anymore. Unless he's a real charmer. *He actually is, but you know what I mean.*

He cooks me dinner, tells me he wants to go out dancing with me. *Thus, meet people he enjoys being with.* Wants to marry me. *Well, that was a joke, but still … was it?* And is so open about everything that I can't help but wonder whether it was *my own cool reaction (and possibly my cancelling two dates at the last-minute?)* to his standing me up that led him to look for a possible replacement. After all, as my soulmate says, "You can be such a ball-breaker", and I truly am a star at scaring people off with my Dutch bluntness. Yeah, well … He did go out chasing again, and he did actively approach 'Tequila', and fuck knows who else. Does he know I am Tequila? Or suspect it? Fuck, indeed. But I was there as well. And I had a reason. Hot Date #1 had stood me up. How dare he! What if he really did go partying, as he said he wished? What if I actually cooled him off after that? I probably did. What if he needed time to think about his situation(s)? Well, he could have told me so. Casual dating is too complicated for me. As I am not casual. Nor partial. I am whole. I am me. Too many feelings to give and too many feelings I need. I do feel for Hot Date #1. I do enjoy spending time with him.

Is this where you get rid of your 'casual'?

I fear that I will wake up and find out it was all just sex, no connection. What the hell am I doing, and why do I go back for more, even though I don't have a real answer to my question? No clue as to what he wants out of all this. But I believe somehow I do. Maybe I shouldn't go back. But why *not* go back as long as he makes me feel so 'alive'? So appreciated as a woman? I am definitely not interested in Hot Date #2. And Hot Date #3 didn't get back to me.

I am doing too much thinking while I should be having fun. *Why do I*

172

feel so conflicted?

The Pursuer is on to me again as well. I didn't call as I had promised, but sent him a last minute text to find out whether he was in town last night. I could have gone for a drink with him before meeting Hot Date #1, but was hoping not to. No reply, so I went for a drink with another friend.

He wrote back this morning that he would be in town on Wednesday. I tell him I have this Dutch event coming up next Sunday, and would he like to join me with a bunch of wild Dutch guys for a drink? He asks if he may come and visit me in my town. I tell him he may, but I would be distracted as when I'm around here I have kids to take care of and projects to work on. So it would be better to meet the Sunday I proposed. At least I would then have time to speak and, above all, listen to him to find out what he wants out of all this. He tells me he will be there, and we will have fun. I am a bit anxious. Will have to invite our mutual friend as well. Another one of my local friends will be there too. And a whole lot of Dutchies. Fellow countrymen will definitely come to the rescue of a 'Maiden in Distress'.

The ghost of lust eats and leaves ...

-Anthony Liccione

Sunday, May 15th 2016

CASUAL DATING FROM A MALE PERSPECTIVE

I spoke with my soul sister this morning on the phone. I wanted to hear her opinion on my writings. She was delighted with what I had come up with so far. She tells me it's the same old story: people have been having affairs since the beginning of time. I agree. But time has somehow changed, and so have people. Their attitudes. Their approaches. She insists that I be careful and not hurt my feelings in the process *("Don't burn your wings")*, as she knows how I'm cut out *(as you do as well, by now)*. I can't speak freely, as my daughter is sitting next to me and the almost-ex is upstairs, so I let her talk. She mentions it would be interesting to follow up on the 'female side' of casual dating that I had begun to delve into this week. She also notices my need of constant recognition. I wish her a pleasant day, and tell her to say Hi to her husband for me.

The woman is right, though. I have been lacking recognition. Without that, I do not function well. I am not complete, and everything I tackle seems to take so much longer. I always think too much about other people and take too little action for myself. Someone once told me that *love implies at least one expectation: to be acknowledged, that our feelings be acknowledged. Without that, everything slowly fades away.* I know for a fact that I do. I need someone to love me unconditionally, someone who thinks the world of me. I deserve it, because I do my share of the work to make it happen. But in the end, it always takes two.

I have changed over the last couple of months. I have been working hard to reclaim my independence, and I am happy with myself. It shows. People now see me for who I am. Not for what I am.

Oh, my God!

No wonder some men talk the way they do when they approach Tequila on the site. It's trash at it's purest. Gutter-talk. What kind of women are these? I mean, who advertises her hugely suggestive arse in a profile picture? Or a (suggestive) blow-jobbing mouth? Or breasts? Few women upload a 'profile picture'. You know . . . profile as in *a face*! How can any woman present herself like that as an introduction to a potential (even if casual) lover? It feels cheap. Meat-market style. The style in which the messages I received were written. Not suggestive. No. They literally tell you what they want to do to you, or what they want you to do to them; how they will go about it, and when. I am not naïve. Not at all. But this is not how I ever imagined profiling myself on line. WOW! How is any weak man going to resist that?

I feel sick. I want to vomit.

When I was told women were aggressive on the site, I understood their approach was aggressive. Though this was the case for some, not all initiated the contact. But when a man did, they replied. The way they did it! These women know what they want and how, and even tell men when. They dictate and use their all to get it. Dirty *(read: foul)* language included. *Ah, but Mac was like this—is this why Hot Date #2 talked dirty? Because he believes that women will like him if he talks like that?* I thought *I* was a predator when I was young. But I was *nothing* compared to this. Just a deer. A lame though witty teenager with a healthy appetite for sex. Full stop. When I know what I want, I do my utmost to get it. But on my terms. I will *not* sell myself short. Hey, women out there! Are we the same race? Have you no class whatsoever? Yet another species in the animal kingdom? Internet flower-power? Sexual liberation?

This quote from Hunter S. Thompson seems appropriate:

I was not proud of what I had learned

but I never doubted that it was worth knowing.

Remember I told you earlier I was CEO of a multi-million company? Well, long before that, as you can imagine, I was a regular employee. The very first time I took a client out for wining and dining, I was requested to drop him off later at the airport. The client hinted that it all depended on me: he was either going to fly back that night, or the following morning (*See? I could have been a mistress a long time ago*). He flew back that same night. And I drove like a bat out of hell to a friend/colleague (*whom I slept with at the time*) to ask for advice. I knew I had to entertain clients, but was I supposed to sleep with them? I just didn't want to find myself in situations like this. He was not surprised, and told me that some women in our line of business did not hesitate to sleep with clients if horizontal business meant good business. At 26, I was shocked. I had never considered myself to be naïve. I only wanted merit for the good job I delivered, and not closing a deal because I would sleep with a client. I never took another client out for dinner for the rest of my career. Lunches worked out just fine. This particular client ceased to work for that company not long after our dinner. I do not know why. But I did a lot of business with that same company after he left. Probably *denying* sex to a client influences your business as well . . .

Although the attitude of these women makes me sick, I can't help wondering why I cannot be *a tiny bit* more like them. I'm talking about the 'no-feelings', 'sex-only' approach, not the pictures they advertise themselves with. Nor the foul language they use. Because that's all it takes, doesn't it? It does. Well, I am not like that. I am not the 'just-sex' type of girl. Not cut out to be a porn queen. And I feel *too fucking much*. I've had it.

I am no longer interested. And now, it is for good. I start feeling desperate. Why? Because I tried to find out what makes women sign up to casual dating sites; half expecting the bored housewife or the woman not ready for commitment. But definitely not the desperate bitch-search for sex. Upon asking them questions like what they want/expect from registering on this site, all you receive is cheap dirty language ... not one decent conversation came out. I wish I had never approached this side of the parallel world that I was so interested in learning about. Of course I know these women exist, but I am extremely disappointed that even a decent 'man' *(me)* is replied to in an indecent manner. I will try to gather more information from other men on this subject, for the one I now receive first-hand is making me feel truly sick. To think I was amongst these women on the same site ... And that Hot Date #1 would see me as he saw them ...

And I thought I could handle it all . . .

It doesn't help that the almost-ex was trying to pick a fight earlier. Not tonight, he won't. I tell him that he can think what he likes, say what he wants, but as far as 'we' are concerned, he cannot get me any lower. I hit bottom a long time ago. He makes me feel as if I had failed in many things throughout my life. And that is simply false. I was hugely successful. In many ways. I had a flourishing business, a *lot* of money, the cars, the house, the jewelry, my kids, my studies, and, to top it off, I threw in a marathon. Fuck you, Hubby! What did *you* accomplish in these years?

I wrote earlier that I did a lot of introspection when I realized my marriage was over at the end of last year. It dawned on me that I had lost my main rock, my husband, for good. My marital relationship was not ever going to be right again. But I had my 3 beautiful (unknowing but 'still-feeling-the-situation') kids and my soul sister to support me, and I hung on to them for dear life. After the maelstrom from feeling so high to feeling so low in the space of a few weeks, I now believe I've lost my balance. Does this mean that my stability depends on the rocks available to me? Do I need to cling to *someone* to be happy and high? I do have the urge to belong *with* someone. I was in dire need of acceptance and praise. Any. But that has changed as well. I will no longer be needing anyone. I have my friends. I have my kids. I have my projects. I simply am. Full stop. No needing. And it feels so good …

Hot Date #1 gives me hot sex and a break for discussion. That's enough for my sex drive. But in the long run, it will not be enough. It *was* just for a while, while I was with him, as if under a spell. But the spell is broken when the door closes behind me. It doesn't help that he didn't text today. Too many 'duties', I guess.

Polite as I am, I write Hot Date #3, Bad, that I am signing out, as the casual dating site is not 'doing it' for me. I tell him I felt he was somehow different, and I would still be interested in meeting him. He has my e-mail if he wants to contact me.

As usual, I am with high hopes but low expectations.

So much emotion in motion ...
Sometimes isolation is all one needs to recover.

Monday, May 16th 2016
FEELING BETTER

I am surprised by a lot of the things I do and say lately. I shouldn't be, because deep inside I've always been *the Artist* in the family. The odd one. 'Diva', they called me when I was young. I accepted the title, as it may have been the right one at the time. I have always been quite expressive, emotional, loud, and a bit out of touch with reality. I prefer Artist over Diva.

Make-up, fashion, and all the things that teenagers want, I've never been really interested in. I wore mascara. Just that. I did try out many things, but even today, if I do not have client meetings (or a Hot Date), all I use is a crème and mascara. Never ever do I wear make-up. When I was 18 and short skirts with high heels were in fashion, I used to cut off my jeans to turn them into shorts, and wore a shirt and mountain shoes to go with them. I danced on the piano, though. I drank (a lot) with the guys, and smoked dope every now and then. I experimented. I never had a lot of girlfriends. I found them annoying. I preferred to have one best friend (female) and a lot of male mates. Is that why today my intuition is on alert? Do I know them too well? Should I have gone out more with girls so as to learn their games?

Anyway, I got up early this morning and the sun was shining. My day starts off well with a morning walk with darling dog. Especially 'cause the sun is out.

I started reading a book and finished it on the same day. 405 pages. I just couldn't put it down. It's called *Not if I See You First.* It made me laugh, it made me cry, and I feel all sassy. A 'feel good' book. My daughter felt sorry for me, as I was crying over my reading.

No texting from Hot Date #1. But then again, I didn't expect anything from him. Not after the 'duty' mention from Friday night. I have decided I will leave him be today. I talk too much. I feel too much. Can't and don't want to deal with that right now.

I now have to concentrate on a job interview I have on Thursday, and I want this to be *the* job. I also have to finalize a contract for the web development of one of my projects and call back a client on the theme of this year's festival, for which I have to come up with exclusive VIP-room decoration material. *Mmm, can do with a VIP right now.* And I will chase the owner of the house I am after since December. Finally, find more artwork for my projects.

All excited about everything that's happening right now!

> "Hi, hope you are ok, sleep well 😌 😴"
>
> "Yeah, I'm well 😊 how was your weekend w/ the girls? Did something nice? Sweet dreams 😴"
>
> "Was nice, Gracias, I am already in bed closing my eyes 😊 See you soon 😴"
>
> "Don't put pictures in my head, Señor 😌"

Friends with benefits?
Don't sample the goodies
unless you are willing to risk
addiction and withdrawal.

-Ann Landers

Tuesday, May 17th 2016

THE SUN SHINES JUST FOR ME

It's still cloudy when I leave the house this morning at 07h00, but when I arrive at my favourite spot by the lakeside, the sun breaks through straight on my face, as if to say, 'Wake-up, life is beautiful, and I'm here to keep you warm!' Warm, of course, being an overstatement, as it is mid-May and I am still wearing my winter jacket in the morning. But hey, the sun is right. Life *is* beautiful, and I am alive. I sit down and have a cigarette. I dream about my projects, and the job I so desperately want. I take some pictures. The reflection of a building on the water with three yellow buoys floating … I find it symbolical, and send a copy to Hot Date #1 wishing him a pleasant day. I decide that this is the last message. Enough with the texting. No more pictures in the morning. I will see him again, but on my terms, not his. Every Tuesday. Yoga. Maybe one more evening if proposed and I'm free. *Sex on Legs always gets what she wants, right?* I try to shut down whatever feelings I had, as I intend to continue enjoying our time together.

I have moved on to another site. I am skeptical, but willing to wait this one out. My name is now Cassie. The rest remains the same. Already 5 contact requests; only one of interest, as he clearly states that he is looking for a long-term 'relation'. I ask for a picture and inform him that I've found his 'out-of-the-ordinary' writing quite appealing, and may be interested in furthering the exchange. I offer him to send me his picture by e-mail, as he may not wish to post it on the site.

You have 3 choices in life:

Give up

Give in

Or give it all you got

I guess I'm the 'give it all' type of girl. Research continues. Let's find me someone looking for a real 'mistress' as per my definition. ☺

But first, work to do ...

I have a long 'conversation' on Messenger with the Pursuer. He seems to be quick at getting back on his feet. New top job, cleaned-up family issues, seems concerned for a friend and is wanting to help him (*but he doesn't*). And he's pushing to meet with me. I tell him we will meet Sunday (*amongst a bunch of 'wild' Dutch*), and inform him that I invited our mutual friend as well. Told him I was quite selective in my choice of friends, and if he knows how to behave himself I may decide to meet again. But only if we keep it fun and distant. He says he can hold himself back. *LOL.* We'll see . . .

The nice man from the new site has already sent his picture. He looks like the almost-ex. Guess that's a no-go. How do you tell someone he looks like your husband and that is the reason you don't want to meet up with him? *I guess you just tell him he looks like your husband, and that's why you don't want to meet up.* Done.

Hot Date #1 texts that he is very tired and has to get up early the following morning, so no sex that night. *Didn't count on it, hon. Plus you're there and I'm here, and I don't do phone sex.* And how was my day. I inform him that it was excellent, and that everything is coming together nicely, all at the same time. And that I'm happy. I also tell him I am to meet with the girls tonight at 21h00. *So get on with it, will you?* He would like to see me on Thursday. I tell him I am not available, as meetings are planned. I can do tomorrow or Friday this week. *Or both, but of course don't tell him that.* He insists on that with the early start he would be tired tomorrow, unless I want to do all the work (with a winking smiley) … I let him know that I'm on a high and can handle the whole world at the moment, and that it's up to him. Also tell him I'll bring him propolis next week. *Why am I being so fucking nice?* BTW, the shower gel is divine. I tell him that I'm running late, as usual, and I must go. Ask him to confirm whether tomorrow or Friday. Sleep well, with a kissing smiley. We'll leave that to tomorrow . . .

I hope it's becoming clear to him that I don't need him to have fun, but that I choose to meet with him for fun *if and when* I'm available. Up till now he had been driving me crazy. Let's turn the tables. *You want to play, Hot Date #1?* Let's play.

Received an e-mail on the Tequila account from Dude. *Guess he's had his share of sex-craving bitches over the weekend* . . . Tell him I would like to see his picture first, and if interested would send him mine. Also informed him that I would be in his area on Thursday, if he cared to meet. BTW, I've changed my interest to 'long-term sex relation' on the Cassie account. Let's hope they do not *all* look like my husband. ☺

Maybe the mistress part plays out there? Exciting!

Recognition is different than love …

I needed to be seen.

Wednesday, May 18th 2016
BUSY DAY

So far, it has been a busy week between prepping tomorrow's job interview, and travelling for my projects. Below is today's texting with Hot Date #1 in between meetings and flights:

> "I'm sorry honey. I fell asleep. This week is hard, as I have to get up at 05:00 every day . . . Have a nice day 😗"

> "OK, tough . . . Cold showers it is . . . Miss you, handsome . . . Enjoy your day 😁"

> "Or . . . How about this: I'll arrive there for 19h00, you have a shower, I'll make you dinner; you make coffee (as I fuck up your machine, otherwise), we talk a bit, I give you massage (but only if you can handle it w/out getting sexy), and I'm out by 09h00. No sex (will be hard, but I've taken worse)."

> "Now that's me being nice for a hardworking man . . . 😊"

> "Haha, you're sweet. Tomorrow would be superb" *(wtf, didn't I make it clear enough that I was not available?)* "around 20h00, what do you think? 😁" *(I think I should start looking for a serious replacement)*

> "Voilà, landed . . . OK, will cancel my friend . . ." *(why do I give in?)* "Want me to bring food? Sex or no sex? If latter, need to put on non-sexy knickers and have a cold shower 😊"

> "Haha, bring everything. Food, sex, and yourself. 20h00 ok for you? Was on the sofa. Everything ok? 😗"

> "Mmmm had a bath . . . Feel all rosy & sexy . . . Yeah, travelled, was in Amsterdam today. Good meetings & cloudy weather 😊 How was your day? You must be tired. Well . . . You had the possibility to fall asleep w/ a massage tonight 😊 I'm off to bed—excited for tomorrow 😗 😗 Sleep well macho-man 😁"

"Hehe, you're really sweet" *(and don't you forget that, señor)*, "yeah, day was good, a lot of work but ok. Also off to bed. Sweet dreams, hasta mañana 😚 😚 😚 💀"

"Hasta mañana, Señor 😚"

"☺️ 😊"

No reply from Dude. What do these men want?

And Hot Date #1 has picked up on Tequila again . . . Let's try and find out tomorrow night what makes him tick. *If only sex with Hot Date #1 wasn't so good . . .*

If you want something you've never had,
you've got to do something you've never done …

-Unknown

Thursday, May 19th 2016
JOBS, HOUSES, LOVER-BOY

Extremely 'hype' today. Interview prepping, shower, make-up, dress (sexy, but professional).

> "Buenos días, bella, have a beautiful day 😊 😳"

> "Merci, adrenaline kicks in 😖 not good for tuches 🥴 On my way . . . CU tonight 😘 😘"

The interview takes almost 2 hours. Time that I didn't notice passing, as it was extremely interesting. Do hope to get this job. Nice company, nice people, and a start-up, so lots of things to develop. New and exciting. On my way back, I meet with the website students. Requirements are coming together, and we can start doing some real developing soon. Projects going in the right direction.

Got an e-mail for an interesting house. I arranged a visit for the following day. If the job goes through and the house is nice, it's mine. New life, new projects. I feel wonderful and excited. Let's see what Hot Date #1 has in mind . . .

It was a mistake,
you said.
But the cruel thing was,
it felt like the mistake was mine...

For trusting you.

-David Levithan

Monday, May 23rd 2016
HOT DATE #1, Part . . . (I lost count)

It's been a busy couple of days. Job interview on Thursday, meeting Hot Date #1, visiting a house, meeting with a bunch of Dutch people on Saturday evening, and again with another group of Dutchies on Sunday evening. With a no-show by the Pursuer, -which I didn't miss out on,- as I had no expectations whatsoever. And the weather was sunny and beautiful, so I greatly enjoyed my weekend.

Upon arriving on Thursday evening, I place a phone call to my home country from the car. Dad's birthday. I am slightly early ... *but hadn't I made it a point never to arrive at the arranged hour?* This somehow seems important to me. I don't know why . . .

Hot Date #1 always opens the door, but never waits *at* the door for me. He's always in the living room. Almost as if he wants to check me out as I come in. Preying on me before he kisses me and I jump him. I am all excited because of the interview that went extremely well, and I tease him that maybe now he has to do long weekends in the town where I had the interview, as his girlfriend lives there as well. I drop the groceries in the kitchen, and he's surprised that I am actually going to cook for him. *So am I, as he's now purely Sex-god to me, right?* But I do need some food in my stomach, as I have not eaten all day. I take his hands and place them on my breasts. W*ow, nipples, steady. Cooking comes first.* He mentions that we could have called for pizza. I say that it is nothing extraordinary, basic pasta with bear's garlic, oil and walnuts, and a tomato-cucumber salad. He wants to help, and I have him cook the pasta while I prepare the rest. I feel a bit awkward, as I don't want to open all cabinets to find what I need. And a bit nervous as well, as this was the first time I cooked for him and wanted it to be perfect. OK, at least good. He says he needs a woman to organize his kitchen. All the while, kissing in between actions, or actions in between kissing, depending on how you may look at it. I wouldn't mind cooking like

193

this more often. Exciting.

We actually manage to eat before having sex. That is a first . . . And we have coffee as well. He wants to see the artistic work I've been doing so far. *Waste of time, Hot Date #1. Let's get on with it, shall we?* Funny how he now knows so much more about my work and what makes me tick than I know about him. Whenever I ask how his day was, what he has done that day, he replies that it was either busy or quiet, but not much more. So still no clue as to what he is actually doing, except that his company is part of a large national chain. We talk about job interviews and experiences we've had interviewing. And I feel he's in a completely different world than I am. That does not bother me, as I enjoy his company. However, I do feel a bit sorry for his girlfriend, as I have the impression he's leading her on. *Is she rich? And how does she do it, leaving him be for 7 fucking years? She definitely is Acing in patience (with a capital A, of course)!*

Tasting my cooking, he mentions again he should marry me, to which I reply that that would never ever happen, as he is unable to live with someone. He is to much of an einzelgänger, not in the bad sense of the word, but too fond of the freedom of not having to answer for the hours spent away from his partner. Too much of a womanizer and not willing to give all that up. He only looks at me, and doesn't reply. Almost as if realizing I am right and my insight cannot be challenged . . . Did I make him see that I understood? He tells me to make myself comfortable and relax. *Really, Hot Date #1. Driving half an hour to relax? Don't want to relax, I want sex. Preferably now.* Right. Why do I bother to dress the way I dress, as everything is off in no time, anyway? He doesn't seem to care about lingerie either. He *is*, however, sometimes interested in checking out my stockings. But they're off really fast as well. And why the make-up? I should try it on more Hot Dates, as not even Estée Lauder resists Sex-god's lovemaking. And I tell you that he's not even licking my face to take it off . . .

194

Sex is good with Hot Date #1. But short that night. He's tired. I call him old man again, which by the look on his face is not a welcomed remark. *Well, Hot Date #1, that's what you get when involved with more than one woman. Deal with it!*

It's hard to let go and leave, as I haven't had enough yet. *Nymphomaniac in the making?*

"Nice dreams 😊 😘"

"Home safe—sweet dreams 💗"

"Your spirit flows out of your body

As a creature of light, you travel through the universe and dive into existence

Because you can see the infinity of becoming

In warm waves you can feel the never-ending stream of life

You recognize the eternal truth of the universe

At the origin of being, everything runs together to begin again

There are no opposites and no differences

Everything is one"

-Unknown

"I believe that sums up how my body feels when having sex w/ you. I am whole. Thank you. Enjoy your day 😘"

"Buenos días, Bella, I assume you slept well . . . Enjoy your day 😁"

"Hola, Señor—noooo, extremely restless . . . Not enough sex, I think 😊 but feeling good anyway 😊 don't work too hard 😘"

"Wish you a wonderful w/end. See you soon 😊 😙"

"Hola, hombre, was half asleep . . . Guess last week packed me in 😊 You knock me off my feet, Señor . . . Enjoy your w/end 😙"

"Gracias 😊 😳"

No texting till this morning. Weekends still off-limits for communication. No worries. Was too busy with my Dutch mates anyway . . .

Friends with benefits?
Forget it!

Friends with batteries,
and a lot less drama!

Tuesday, May 24th 2016
A WOMAN SHOULD HAVE

These are some of the topics addressed by the insightful women who contributed to *30 Things Every Woman Should* Have *and Should* Know *by the Time She's 30,* from the editors of *Glamour* and Pamela Redmond Satran (Hyperion, April 4, 2012):

A WOMAN SHOULD HAVE . . . one old boyfriend she can imagine going back to and one who reminds her of how far she's come . . .

A WOMAN SHOULD HAVE . . . enough money within her control to move out and rent a place of her own, even if she never wants to or needs to . . .

A WOMAN SHOULD HAVE . . . something perfect to wear if the employer, or date of her dreams wants to see her in an hour . . .

A WOMAN SHOULD HAVE . . . a youth she's content to leave behind . . .

A WOMAN SHOULD HAVE . . . a past juicy enough that she's looking forward to retelling it in her old age . . .

A WOMAN SHOULD HAVE . . . a set of screwdrivers, a cordless drill, and a black lace bra . . .

A WOMAN SHOULD HAVE . . . one friend who always makes her laugh . . . and one who lets her cry . . .

A WOMAN SHOULD HAVE . . . a good piece of furniture not previously owned by anyone else in her family . . .

A WOMAN SHOULD HAVE . . . eight matching plates, wine glasses with stems, and a recipe for a meal that will make her guests feel honoured . . .

A WOMAN SHOULD HAVE . . . a feeling of control over her destiny . . .

EVERY WOMAN SHOULD KNOW . . . how to fall in love without losing herself . . .

EVERY WOMAN SHOULD KNOW . . . how to quit her job, break up with a lover and confront a friend without ruining the friendship . . .

EVERY WOMAN SHOULD KNOW . . . when to try harder . . . and when to walk away . . .

EVERY WOMAN SHOULD KNOW . . . that she can't change the length of her calves, the width of her hips, or the nature of her parents . . .

EVERY WOMAN SHOULD KNOW . . . that her childhood may not have been perfect . . . but its over . . .

EVERY WOMAN SHOULD KNOW . . . what she would and wouldn't do for money or love . . .

EVERY WOMAN SHOULD KNOW . . . how to live alone . . . even if she doesn't like it . . .

EVERY WOMAN SHOULD KNOW . . . whom she can trust, whom she can't, and why she shouldn't take it personally . . .

EVERY WOMAN SHOULD KNOW . . . where to go . . . be it to her best friend's kitchen table . . . or a charming inn in the woods . . . when her soul needs soothing . . .

EVERY WOMAN SHOULD KNOW . . . what she can and can't accomplish in a day . . . a month. . . and a year . . .

Something to think about. It was mentioned that every woman should know all the above before the age of 30. Did I? I still have a hard time letting go, although I know the time has come. I am talking about my marriage *and* about Hot Date #1.

I read a text last week that made me feel truly sad,

"So, here you are

too foreign for home

too foreign for here.

Never enough for both"

As Hot Date #1 is, like myself, a foreigner in this country, I believe he may feel the way I do when reading this quote. By the way, it's from Ijeoma Umebinyuo. I decide that I want to share this with him this morning.

"My philosophy for this morning's walk . . . And so true for all those who've lived away from their country long as we have. Bit sad, right? Enjoy your day 😌"

"Yes, that's right, it's very sad 😊 Tonight @ 20h00 still ok for you? 😁"

"Si, Señor 😊"

"Good, I am looking forward to you 😁"

"You better rest then . . . 😌 Need me to bring something? "

"Only yourself 😊 😁"

"Haha—all zen and dressed for yoga? 😜"

"That's good, haha 😬 hasta mas tarde 😁"

Over lunch, I receive a new message from Dude. He writes nicely, and asks me why I haven't replied to him. Did I find a lover in the meantime? Had he been offensive in his approach? I let him know that I like his writing style and that I did reply, even had suggested I was in his town last week . . . That I clearly understood his intentions, and that mine were similar minus the husband approval, as this was a soon-to-be ex-husband. Also stress again that I am definitely not interested in a new husband/boyfriend, as I am neither ready nor have the time for this. Ask him again for his pictures. Maybe I should have mentioned I want the experience of being someone's mistress. If I were a man, would that turn me on? Yes, I believe that would caress my masculinity . . . *I'll tell him face-to-face* . . . Let's see if he writes back first and how. Is this the guy I could be 'mistress' to?

Articles keep popping up about women's menopause. *Mine started early at approximately 45-46, so I guess I'm almost through. No more hot flashes.* They say women over 50 have a lower or non-existent sex drive . . . They are so missing out on that extraordinarily sexy and fulfilled feeling you will have only if you've had good sex. *They should all be treated with a Hot Date #1.*

Or maybe it's the abstinence for 1.5 years that did the trick? Interesting . . .

In the meantime, I have started this discussion on Facebook to find out whether a penis is a man's best friend . . . I guess FB is too public to pour your heart out about your penis . . . But some interesting observations came back.

The first reaction was (of course) from my twin sister, who said that her penis is without doubt her best friend. Upon which I asked her: 'Transexual'? Her reason was that she could take him anywhere, and he always stood to attention when she was around. *She's talking about her fucking vibrator!*

201

The second reaction is a question on whether my pussy is *my* best friend. I answer that I have a tigress but that that was not the information I was after, so what about it? He says, "To be honest, no. It's a nice tool, which comes in handy from time to time—if you're lucky." He's still young, though. He'll find out sooner or later that there's no such thing as luck.

Yet another reader tells me that it is his best friend by 80%, and his worst enemy by 20% (as it will give his feelings away).

Furthermore, someone writes that a man's penis is close to being a best friend to his wife, but not to him. I ask him what this appendix of pleasure means to *him*. Laughing, he replies that it's his playmate, toy-boy, soulmate (almost his best friend). I also laugh, and ask, 'A penis with a brain?', to which he replies, 'Uh . . . I guess sometimes it does have it's own thoughts.' Needless to say, Wicked Willy immediately comes to mind.

A friend from Vegas agrees with my assertion that men put unusual emphasis on their packages, partly because they must touch their penis so often during the day (patting it down in the morning, placing it comfortably in their underpants before putting on jeans, urinating). He also mentions that no matter how well-endowed a man may be, from his perspective (always looking down to his own member, thus having a foreshortened view), what he sees is 30-40% shorter than the actual length. That difference is also made evident when he glances over at his neighbor, where his perspective is accurate. Depending on how you look at it, a man could logically experience some insecurity, as there is always a very discreet comparison when the opportunity arises. Men frequently give a name to their penis, and always handle it with fondness. As it sometimes acts of its own accord, men are constantly aware of their member. So the answer is YES, the penis is a man's best friend!

It must be hard for a man to carry this 'obligation' to please his woman/women. One experiment that I cannot carry through. And no, I have not one lesbian chromosome in me, so a strap-on won't do!

Let's try to get some more work done, then shower and off to Hot Date #1 a.k.a. Sex-god . . .

Never get too comfortable.

There is always room for improvement or replacement.

Wednesday, May 25th 2016
HOT DATE #1 . . .

"Honey 😳 can you please bring a bottle of Coke? Gracias
😙"

"No problema, hombre 😊 Your wish is my command (but I
do have limits 😌)"

"I know, I'm washing 😌 😷 😷 😷" *(Washing what, hombre?
Yourself? With my shower gel? Could have waited a bit
then . . .)*

"Ah non . . . You know nothing about my limits 😌" *(he can't
possibly know what I don't know myself yet, can he?)*

As usual, he is in his living room, observing me, preying on me as I enter. He asks me about my limits, to which I reply that that is for him to find out. I look sex-on-legs, and I know it. Press-button denim mini-dress, skin-tight. High-heeled boots up to my knees, not sexy but cool. And matching purse. A 'wow !' escapes from his lips before he kisses me. *Sweet Lord . . .* I hand him his Coke to stop him, warning him that it may be a bit shaken *(Coke not being the only thing that's shaken, though)* and that he should be careful when opening it. He asks me if I am hungry, to which I bluntly reply, 'Yes, for sex with a Hot Cuban.' He laughs.

We talk and drink *(Cuba Libre, what else?)* and, as always, end up mentioning his inexhaustible sex drive. This is getting a bit boring, right? Get on with it, Hot Date #1. Don't talk about it, do it! I am getting impatient.

We have sex for close to 4 hours with a small break for drinks and a cigarette. He tells me we're one of a kind, and I think to myself,

Definitely in bed, but we're nothing alike outside the sack. Not only does he need a lot of sex, but also different partners, or so I am led to believe. I know he enjoys having me, but I also *think* he may need diversity. Everything is contradictory with him. One night, he wants to teach me to dance so we can go out; another night he wants to marry me; yet another night he cooks dinner for me and proposes to come with me to New Orleans, a city I had mentioned was on my bucket list. He shows me Cuba through his stories. I didn't ask for any of this. What's next?

I guess I'm *in love with making love* to this man. Without knowing a lot about him, which is why it's so hard to let go. I'm not ready to let go: I need to know more and will most definitely not give up good sex in exchange for mediocrity. This is addictive. He is addictive. And 'good' doesn't even come close to defining sex with Hot Date #1.

I always did like sex, but having anything between 3 to 6 orgasms per 'yoga' session . . . I believe the last time that happened, I was young, wild, and free. And now, I don't wish to let go of the feelings that come with it. I want it as much as I can have it, for this intense feeling may never again be repeated.

Perturbing. Have to work harder to find a replacement.

> "Nice dreams, hoping to see you next time 😴"
>
> "Home safe 😚 Sweet dreams, hombre . . . Not sure to be able to hold myself till next Tuesday, though . . . 😌"

Communication must be HOT:

Honest
Open
Two-way

-Dan Oswald

Sunday, June 12th 2016
I'M BACK

Still meeting with Hot Date #1 every Tuesday, and sometimes Fridays. I'd like to turn this into 'friends with benefits', but somehow don't seem to be able to make myself trust him fully. You understand why.

Although we talk a lot *(before, in between, and after sex rounds)*, I'm not sure where this is leading to. Last Friday night was extraordinary. But his ego was a bit dented when I told him I couldn't let go of myself 100%. That I really needed to be in love to be able to do that.

I've done a lot of soul-searching *(again . . . it doesn't stop, does it?)* in the last 2 weeks. I'm smitten with making love to this man, but it is no longer enough for me. He's not all that forthcoming for me to fully trust. I've been as open as I could at this stage. Except for all my doings within the casual dating world, of course. That's none of his business, inasmuch as his girlfriend of 7 years is none of mine. I've been able to switch off the 'feeling' button, and, as far as I am concerned. whenever I go to his place I'm on an extremely fulfilling sex-date. With a highly sexy and streetwise guy. Although his attitude still makes me wonder, I am not really too bothered as to the why anymore. I simply enjoy.

I have been in contact with 3 other men lately. No sex as of yet. But potentially interesting. Two of them in particular.

I don't have trust issues ...

I just know better.

Wednesday, June 22nd 2016
THE MORNING AFTER

Arriving at Hot Date #1's place last night, I have a hard time not to jump him immediately. 1.5 weeks without sex is now unthinkable. I missed him, and I let him know it. He tells me I look great, that I lost weight. *Thank you, Señor. All there to please you.*

We drink, I eat mangos, he eats cheese, we smoke. I brought him some bracelets from my last trip, and hand him 75 pages of my book. As promised. He's surprised, and I tell him to burn the pages after reading them: he doesn't want someone else (*girlfriend or daughters*) to find them while in his possession.

Somehow, he seems touched. *What am I trying to accomplish with this?* I'm handing over my feelings. What will he do with them? Will he understand that this is about me, and although he plays an important role in the story, it is not about him at all? Will he care that I trust him with my feelings? Or will he put the pages aside as a 'nice tale' the way he did when I sent him my report on the squirrel and my dog? Too late now, as he's now got my writing. We'll see.

It's hard to keep my hands to myself while with him in the same room.

I am not treated the way I deserve. Yet I come back for more. Again and again. Am I becoming a masochist?

He invites me to his bedroom, and another marathon starts. Hot . . .

At some point, I have to tell him to stop, to really stop. I panic and force him to stop! He's getting too close for my comfort, as he was about to have 'all of me'.

Have you ever enjoyed a cervical orgasm? I find it hard to explain, as it may be different for you . . . The way I feel it is that you die and are reborn. I've heard that the cervix is the reflexology point for the heart. Climaxing on cervical stimulation will stir deep feelings of love, spiritual-like, almost like a transcendence. This orgasm spreads all over your body first, and then just explodes. Like a trillion tiny electric shocks touching every nerve. Mind-blowing. And it can keep going for a long period. I break down completely. I pass out. Once, I was extremely emotional and cried for hours. Other times, I felt high on a never-ending wave. And believe me, it's hard to drive your car when that happens.

That sums it up for me. I need to be sure my partner will be there to catch me, and that he is able to meet this need, to give me this comfort, this security I seek to be safe at that unique moment. There have been only two men in my life who were allowed there. I had almost forgotten that this was possible. I *cannot* give it to just anyone.

God, he scared me.

How the fuck did this happen? How did he manage to get me there? He told me to let go, we only live today, and he wants to see it . . . But I couldn't. I tried to explain that he can have it all, but this truly is the one thing I *cannot* give to him. I believe I was silently crying by then, as he tries to comfort me. But I *want* to explain, as this is something so powerful, so deep in me, I'll be *so* vulnerable that he *has* to understand *he* cannot have that part of me. I don't think he understood. How could he, if he doesn't understand *me?* How could he, if he doesn't understand I simply cannot do casual . . .

One more drink and we hit off for round 2. And it's intense.

This was a bumpy ride, and I almost had a major crash. I get back home late. Really late.

"Good morning, hombre—feeling great 😊"

"Bon appetit, enjoy the sun 😊 😊"

"Gracias—did you manage to take the afternoon off? I could have done with some more sleep; dosed a bit in the sun— preparing now for 2nd job interview—c.u. soon 😋 😋"

"Yes, I'm at home, going to see my girls after. Good luck 😊"

"Nice 😊 Enjoy your girls and the sun 😊 Gracias—feel wonderful, so everything should be ok 😊"

Nothing further that day … Not 'how was your interview'? Nada, niente, rien, nichts.

It's not about sex,
it's about connection.

Thursday, June 23rd 2016
NO EXPECTATIONS, STILL UNHAPPY WITH NO ANSWER

> "Hola, Hombre—can you please not appear in my dreams—
> it's too hot 😌"

I sent that while waiting at the gynaecologist in the morning. No reply all day . . . Early evening, I decide I need to know how to organize myself for Friday night:

> "You ok? "

> "Hola, Bella, was sleeping on the sofa 😊" *(again? does that a lot, doesn't he . . .)* "and you? 😴"

> "Fine . . . Want you 😊 You told me you had problems with your leg muscles, did you see your doctor about it?"

> "No, I hope to next week. I am treating it with a special cream, and it's almost gone."

Then we go on for a bit in Spanish, with a lot of help from Google Translator, which most of the time is a pain in the arse. Apparently, my Spanish is rather good today . . . I'm happy with that. I ask him if he started reading, and he tells me he'll start tonight, but first he'll do some training. 'Keep those muscles coming', I reply. I ask him what's happening tomorrow night, as I need to organize my kids. He says he needs to take care of his girls. *WTF, he had told me he wanted to take me out, as his girls weren't coming till Saturday. Does he even know what he says to whom?*

> " Ok, thought we were going out . . ."

> " Yeah, I'm sorry. Still working on arrangements with my ex. I'll let you know tomorrow." *(you don't really think I'll wait for that, do you?)*

I take a moment to message a friend that I would really really, no, *really really* like to go out with for a drink on Friday . . .

"All right, we'll see. I don't mind if you have the girls—that's always a tender issue 😇 I also don't mind if you wanna go out on your own—but just say so 😗"

"Si, claro 😊"

"Buenos noches, Señor—stay out of my dreams, please . . . 😊😊😗"

"No no, imposible 😛, sleep well, 1000 besos 😊😊"

"Gracias, 😊 start reading?"

"I start now. Am very curious 😛😊"

"My soul sister started and didn't stop till page 120 . . . Hope you get some sleep 😛"

"😊💐💐💐" (really . . . roses? I hate roses . . . one of the many things you don't know about me . . .)

"Call me when finished—curious about your reaction . . . First, because you play a large role at the beginning of the story. Second, well, because you're a hombre 😇"

"Ok 😊"

No call . . . Didn't ask me how my appointment with the gynaecologist went either, nor about my appointment with the plastic surgeon I went to see this afternoon for my leg 'lumps', although I did tell him about this on Tuesday. Talk about being interested in one thing only . . . Do I have to give Hot Date #2 and Hot Date #3 another shot? They can't be more disinterested in my well-being than Cuban Hot Chocolate . . .

What's taken for granted
will eventually be taken away …

Friday, June 24th 2016
HELL & FURY

> "Don't you like my writing? Or are you just taking me for
> granted . . . Either way, not appreciated, Señor …"

> "Heeey, I fell asleep on the couch, reading your book. My heel
> hurts, am staying at home quietly."

Well, fuck you, Señor. First you tell me you wanna take me out and
that maybe a friend will come along, so you will still confirm. Then
yesterday, you didn't seem to remember and did not know yet how you
would arrange with your daughters (*a day before?*); and today, you do
not write me to cancel or confirm. I am *NOT* and will *NEVER* be
your duty! And now that I am angry you're all in the defense? Will not
be bothered with you tonight, hombre. I don't answer his text, but go
for a drink with a friend instead, as I had arranged the previous night.
At least, she does not make me angry. On the contrary, she makes me
laugh . . .

By now, my 3 best friends, whom I see and travel with regularly, are
up to date on 'the affair'—not on every detail, of course, but definitely
on my feelings.

The friend I am now out with wasn't as of yet, and I tell her all,
including the 'going out' part of the story and how furious it makes me
to be 'half' invited and then not even receiving a reply. Her reactions
go from 'stick to the Cuban diet, it suits you' to 'dump the bastard'.
And I think to myself that she may say whatever she likes, but in the
end, it will be up to me, right? We laugh a lot, I am teased some more
on my exploits, and I have two espressos before driving back home.

When I arrive, I write back to Hot Date (still) #1.

"I was out with my friends … Fuck, this note has become longer than meant. Btw, this is definitely not a love letter 😉 If I am with you, it is because I want to (I enjoy the company, not just the sex); I truly like you. But I do not 'need' you … I choose to be with you.

Did not appreciate the silent treatment today at all, and *(while we're at it, Señor)* I don't like 'maybes'. If you ask me to spend time with you, I have to make arrangements. If you back out at the last minute, me no like . . .

I am not a complicated person, and I am happy with little; but I need people to be straight with me and don't fuck me around.

I would like to see more of you (and I do not mean only frequency). Now, I've trusted you with the first part of my book (hope you enjoy it 😊). I believe I wanted to show you I trust you with my feelings *(now I am having second thoughts).* And I would like to trust you with the rest as well. But that is now up to you 😊 *(because honestly, I don't believe you started reading when you said you would. Are you interested at all? You're fucking me around big time … not appreciated)*

And no . . . we're not meant to be in love. I cannot be vulnerable with you. Losing myself right now is simply not an option. I have other issues to finish before moving on.

But still . . . I do care for you *(otherwise, you couldn't have come that close to my cervical, although you were really close this week. Shit, that scared me . . . Maybe one day, maybe not, but not now.)* and I do very much enjoy being with you.

Btw, I'm not going out of the country next week (but that's another story).

Leave you to it . . .

Dulces sueños, Señor 😘"

Voilà. Hopefully, he gets the message. Do not fuck me around. Do not fuck with my feelings.

> "I am reading your book now . . and I cannot stop. Point of view very interesting. It is clear that it is difficult to separate the desire and need without encountering feelings. Thank you so much for your confidence. Sleep well and dream of us. Kiss 😚 😚 😚"

Let me love you a little more
before you are not little anymore

-*Unknown*

Saturday, June 25th 2016
THE INDEPENDENT DAUGHTER

"Buenos días, Bella 😊, hope you slept well with this heat. Thank you again for confiding me with this intimacy in your book. To me, it all seems quite intense, and like you, it surprises me that there are so many people who do not lead the life they want. Never before have I been part of such a story, at least not written about. I enjoyed it tremendously. We'll talk more when we meet. Have a beautiful day, kisses 😊😙😙😙💐"

"Hola, mi amante . . . Hesitated a long time whether I wanted you to read this 😊. Still not 100% comfortable with you reading all this, as it makes me only more vulnerable—which I absolutely don't want to (can't be) right now 🙄. But then thought it only fair and maybe interesting to you to find out how and what another person REALLY feels about you, when with you, sees you. You don't often manage to find that out, right? I'm off to take my daughter to the airport this PM. Wish you a wonderful time with your girls 😙"

"Gracias 😊😆"

"Gracias to you. Interesting chapter in my 'second' life 😊😙"

My little girl (12) is travelling all by herself to visit her grandparents. This was her choice. I would have been happy to pay extra for the Unaccompanied Minor service. But no, she was ready to do this on her own. Including the luggage check-in.

I took her to the airport by train. We checked-in her suitcase, and had a coffee at a café outside the airport. Then did some shopping, and off she went. A bit nervous (although she would not admit it). I am so proud of this independent little woman in the making! She'll get there.

She will have everything she wants, and more. I do hope I am the one capable of teaching her that she is able to, and that she does not have to find out by herself, like me, wasting 12 years of her life to reclaim what was always hers in the first place. I call her a diva, as I myself was called at her age. She's creative and has a wild imagination. *Recognize it?* She's a fighter. Good! I used my time on the train to write some more on the restaurant wagon. I felt the person sitting next to me was watching what I was doing.

When I got home, I find that my son will sleep over at a girlfriend's house, and that my almost-ex is at his cousin's wedding. With my daughter gone off to the sun, I'll be all alone.

> "You busy tonight? All family gone here (except for doggie
> 😊) Wanna go for a drink?" *(or do me in the shower after my run?)*
>
> "Hey, yes, I am with my girls 😊 😘"
>
> "Ok, have fun 😘"
>
> "Gracias y salud 😝 😘"
>
> "Salud?"
>
> "Haha, if drinking a glass of wine, we say Salud . . . Cheers 😝"
>
> "No wine for me tonight, I will go running, have a cold shower 😝 and then have more stories to write" *(all this in fucked-up Spanish, of course, asking if it was correct)* 😊 😘
>
> "Hmmm—don't understand 😳 😝"

He sends me a link to another site mentioning that the most-widely-spoken first language in the EU is German . . .

> "Oh, but my German is ok. I just do not find it a sexy
> language . . . Aargh . . . Fuck it! Google Translate not very

good . . . As I said, run, cold shower, and more stories to write" (before my old brain forgets them 😊) "Have a nice evening, Señor . . . BTW, you were in my dreams again last night . . . Hot . . . 😏"

"Hmmm . . . details? 😊"

"Dreams are very private, Señor . . . But I'll have a dream like that any night . . . It did involve running and sweaty bodies 😇"

"Hey, you can make them real 😈"

"Sure, intend to make all my dreams come true. 😇😇 , or rather 😼😼. It's raining hard here—go running now 😼"

"Good, enjoy 😈"

Later that evening:

"Mmmm, still don't like running, but I'm wet and tired, feels ok . . ."

"Hmm wet? 😜 It's hard, but it's good for you 😈"

"Si, it was raining . . . And don't you start 'wet' on me, Señor, as you won't be able to finish it 😝"

"Don't start if you cannot finish it … 😊 I heard that one before, from you of course."

"Haha . . . Buenas noches, Hombre. I'll have my cold shower now, cause you put sweet images in my head that need to be taken care of. Sweet dreams 😘"

"Gracias, Bella, igualmente 😘"

223

I was going to write a hot quote here.
But then I got orgasmic
and forgot all about it.

Sunday, June 26th 2016
ORGASMIC

"Buenos días, señora 😊, how are you? Kisses"

"Orgasmic 😇 And you?"

"How's that . . . You're masturbating? 😜 Well, thanks . . . I am enjoying tranquility with my girls 😊"

"Haha, feeling sexy, feeling high, feeling orgasmic . . . Wanna play? 😺"

"You're alone? Enjoy yourself 😜"

"Prefer a playmate, but by lack of that . . . 😘"

"Oooh, I think you need an army, hehe 😳"

"Mmmmm . . . Don't think an army is in my fantasy right now . . ."

Nothing more from Cuban Sex-god—it's Sunday and he's with the girls. Enjoy them, hombre. Kids don't stay around forever. If you're lucky, they come back once in a while.

I'll save my sexy feelings for next week so I can explode in his very capable hands. I have a cold shower instead.

Later that evening . . .

"Que tengas una noche agradable, me alegra verte otra vez 😘"

Mmmm, told you it was sexy, being written to in Spanish. However, this one was not very well translated to my taste . . . or maybe I had too much Cuban Adonis on my mind to be wanting to understand . . .

"Don't understand" (and neither does Google 😊)

"Wish you a beautiful evening, look forward to seeing you again 😊 😘 "

"Mmmm gracias, hombre—igualmente 😘 you knock me off my feet . . ."

"Oooh 😊 😘"

"Oooh what . . ."

"That I knock you off your feet, I have company 😘" *(sure you do . . .)*

"Claro . . . Have a good one then 😘"

"Gracias 😘 😘 😘"

"De nada, guapo—I'm writing—talk later 😘"

Growing apart
doesn't change the fact that for a long time
we grew side by side;
our roots will always be tangled.

-Ally Condie

Monday, June 27th 2016
ROOTS

On my morning walk, I send Hot Date #1 a picture of a concrete hand 'growing' around a tree. Symbolic, I find, as with the first part of the book, he now holds the roots of my feelings without knowing where they grow. I do know, however. They're growing to be independent once again. I am a whole person, and most of the things I do, say, or show have a meaning. Señor doesn't 'get' this yet, I believe.

"Buenos días, muchacho 😊"

"Buenos días, Bella, nice picture 😊 I wish you a nice day 😚"

In the afternoon, I meet up with my soul sister on the beach by the lake. She comes by bike, and I go for a run before meeting up. While we talk and laugh on the lakeside terrace, there's a pigeon making a show in front of 2 females. He doesn't stop. He comes back again and again. I say to my friend, 'Look, a Cuban pigeon,' and we explode in laughter. Of course, this needed to be filmed and sent to Hot Date #1 with a mention of Cuban pigeon at the playa . . .

"It appears they want to do something 😜 I'm in bed, resting 😊 😚"

"He wants to and tries for a while, but she's not interested . . . Again in bed? You're getting old, muchacho 😌"

"Sí, parece 😜"

"Yoga tomorrow?"

"Of course 😌"

"Mmmm can't wait . . ."

" 😊 😚 "

"Already had my run, but was fortunate to end up on the

beach with my soul sister who biked down to the playa 😊 😊 I'm happy, always a good time with her . . ."

"Good, enjoy 😊"

"Off for shower and dinner with mi hijo—talk later, hombre 😘"

"Bien 😊"

Later that evening:

"Having a bath, after that I'm off to dreamland 😴 Buenas noches, Señor, sweet dreams 😘"

"Gracias, going to bed soon as well . . . alone 😁" *(why does he feel the need to tell me that?)* "Have to get up at 05h00 tomorrow, lots of work. Sleep well, I look forward to seeing and eating you hahaha 😘 🐱 🐱 🐱"

"Haha, I'll make you dinner . . . You need energy 😊"

"I think so . . . But you don't have to cook. I'll eat something. 20h30 ok for you? 😊"

"Don't like my cooking, Señor? 😁"

"Yes, sure. I'd rather spend our time doing something else 😁"

"Mmmm . . . Hope it tastes as good as my cooking then . . . 😘 😘 Sueños salvajes 😺 😺"

"Haha gracias 😘"

That which consumes your mind,
controls your life.

Tuesday, June 28th 2016
FEELINGS

I sent the '1 minute of wisdom' video of José Mujica (former president of Uruguay) with a mention that he's a wise man. It all comes down to mind control.

"Buenos días, handsome 😘"

"Buenos, Bella, wish you a nice day 😊 😴"

Late afternoon:

"PS 20h30 😌 😘"

"Need something?"

"No, gracias 😊"

"Bit late . . . sorrryyyy 😌 leave in 5"

"Yeah, no stress, am home having a Cuba Libre 😛"

Our life is a painting colored by apprehension and desire.

Wednesday, June 29th 2016
APPREHENSIVE

We had cognac to start with. This is a special drink to him, and tonight was a special occasion. Trust. Talk book.

He likes 'our' story and the way I write. I set him straight by the fact that it is my story, not ours: he's only a very important passerby.

He tells me that he is flattered by the way I wrote about him. He'd like to know what makes him so special. I tell him everyone is special to someone. I don't go into details. Not now.

He thanks me again for trusting him with my intimacy. He tells me there are many ways of being 'in love'. And I try to explain the doctor—love—thankfulness—recognition relation. While sitting down with our drinks and cigarettes, he tells me that he's not 'in love', but has feelings for me. He likes me a lot, and not just for the wild hours of sex. He enjoys talking and listening to me ... quite a lot actually.

Communication problems with regards to dinner, hot kisses, and touching in the kitchen. He says he can smell me and wants to have me.

He tells me the look in my eyes is different somehow ... something wrong?

Yes. Something is completely off . . . I realize I don't want this 'sex only' thing anymore. Neither without nor with feelings. It's just not enough for me anymore.

Without answering his question, I tell him of my meeting with the plastic surgeon, who would like to schedule the operation (2.5-3 hours) for the middle of next month. I cannot be bothered: I am not ready for another operation. It upsets me. I've had enough of those already. I feel like crying, and that would be a turn-off, right? If I start, I won't stop, and I'll probably run away. I'm strong. I'm amazing. I'm me. He can think what he likes. But on the inside, emotions like a thunderstorm. WTF?

Intense sex. The connection I seemed to feel is somehow lost after a short while, even during the act.

While engaged, he takes me in his arms and asks what it would take for me to have a man like him, considering the way we met. I tell him I wrote about that. It would be difficult for me on the trust side. Trust is *never* a given, trust can and should be earned. We don't talk about it much, but this has been on my mind a lot today.

What does he mean by 'a man like him'? What traits is he thinking of ? He told me once that his father had had mistresses. Maybe Hot Date #1 should ask his mother how she felt about that. If in love with her husband, she must have been in such desperate pain. How did she survive that? I know I could not. If that's the kind of man he means, the kind that sleeps around because he needs diversity or needs to prove his manhood over and over again, then I don't want that kind of man.

And now that I know of this parallel world, I understand that any man and any woman can do what we do. And it is all so discreet. What woman or man our age with marital or sex issues has *not* done this?

Then what *do* I want in a man? First of all, I do not believe in *having* someone (unless we're talking sex). You are together *with* someone because you both choose to be. Because you are able to please each other, you develop projects together, and you laugh a lot. I would need to be deeply in love, and this has to be mutual. To me, being with a person 'like' Hot Date #1 (to answer *his* question) is equivalent to wanting to be with any other man with a healthy sex drive. I think he would have to work hard to gain my trust (if I were aware of his past escapades while in a relation); always tell me the truth, even if that may hurt; not ever fuck me around; and he would have to guarantee exclusivity. It has to be only me. But to be *with* a man again, *in love* again, I would need to know him better first . . .

Maybe I should turn around the question and ask him what it would take for a man to be with me.

He's the one in need of a break … weird. We end up having a Cuba Libre and smoking. I wanted to eat an apple and a some chocolate, but the apple was disgusting and the chocolate was all melted. Weak from hunger and exhaustion, we ended up ordering pizza. And we hadn't even really started yet.

> "Thank you for your time, sleep well 😊 😘 😘 😘"
>
> "Hope arsehole sleeps well as well 😝 Gracias a ti, hombre 😘"
>
> "😊 😘 🌷 🌷 🌷"
>
> "Home safe 😊 😘 PS I prefer tulips

No amount of guilt
can change the past.
And no amount of worrying
can change the future.

Monday, July 4th 2016
SAY CHEESE

I check my messages on the casual site and there's Jack. Jack would like to know what's behind my (fictional) picture. I check out his pictures. *Mmm... nice, muchacho.* I ask him what he would like to know. He is interested to see what I look like, wants me to tell him what I am looking for. I let him know I would be pleased to send my pictures by e-mail; I am not interested in one-night stands; I would like to get to know him, as he looks nice. *I'm not going to tell him he's 'hot' straight away, right?* He does look like he's got a sense of humour, and maybe a touch of cynicism? I like his picture. He wants high-standard meetings, whatever that may mean.

Now, if he talks about endurance, I can do that. But I am not sure he is talking about that, and I am not sure I want to do that. Not with this man. I have not met him, but I feel I know him. I want to meet this man to 'feel' what this is all about.

Once I receive his e-mail address, I send him my pictures with my telephone number. Now that is definitely one of my rules being broken! Never EVER send your telephone number unless you've met the man. He thanks me, and says he'll get back to me.

He calls me later in the afternoon while I am on the road with my daughter. I was caught by surprise because 'casuals' text, they don't call. I tell him I'll call him back later. Of course, my daughter wants to know who this is, as I am speaking in German. I mumble it's a friend of a friend.

Before I get a chance to call him back, I receive another picture of his on my phone. He warns me his English is not so good. I reply later that I speak German, Dutch, English, and French. He asks for another picture.

I cancel a potential hot date, something-or-other Lion. I couldn't be bothered, and I prefer meeting up with a friend in a town close to where Jack lives, so I invite him out for a coffee. *With my friend around, my feelings are safe.* He replies he's still at a convention where he has to please 40 top chefs with his cheese, and he's not sure when he's going to be ready. He makes cheese. I tell him I am late for my meet-up with my friend at 18h00, but he may buy me a drink later in the evening. I also tell him I'm from *the other* 'cheese country'.

I get another picture from his cheese presentation, a 'hi' from the cheeses. Cheesy. I tell him I was once almost married to a cheese maker, and that I love cheese. My cheese maker was 12 years old at the time, and didn't become a cheese maker till he was 18. I was 8. But he doesn't need to know that now.

So I push him. I want to see him. 21h00, or better another day? He says it would be better another day, and he's sorry, as he would have liked to meet me tonight. And he is still waiting for another picture. I tell him no worries, next time . . . And I did send 2 pictures, does he want more? Yes, he does. He starts sending me his pictures. Very provocative. I ask him to not send me the rest, as I do like surprises . . . with an angel smiley. He understands, but sends me 2 more anyway, stating that now he is done.

> "I am with my friend, I leave you to your cheese. This week I'm flexible, but next week really busy. 😳 Not bad, muchacho 😺"

> "Thursday?"

> (I send him a photo of my leg in ripped jeans.)

> "That's the last one. It's more fun meeting me. Have a nice evening 😋"

> "I will (with another picture) 😬"

"Are you still in town? You still owe me a picture 😖 From which cheese country are you?"

"No, already on my way back. Holland. Thursday ok"

"I love Holland 😋 Don't forget to send picture 😉"

"I am driving . . . dangerous . . . already sent . . ."

"I will make you melt 😁 😌"

"Mmmm maybe a drink first?"

"Whatever 😊 drive safe . . . see you soon 💋"

(Another provocative picture arrives on my screen) "So that you will not fall asleep."

"Hahaha . . . Back home safe . . . Thursday ok for me. What town do you live in exactly? Or meet somewhere halfway?"

(We establish the town where we will meet.)

"Perfect. Are you always this fast? 😊 And now I want another picture!"

"Can't have it. I am Dutch. Very open-minded and extremely direct. When I see what I like . . . what's the use of waiting? But as I said before, I am not interested in one-night stands. I am a 'feelings' person. If I like what I feel when meeting you, I prefer long hot sex instead of telephone/chat sex. So, I will not send you more pictures—you can judge for yourself when we meet. 'If you want it, work for it. It's that simple'."

"I established that . . . direct and open . . . I like that. Ok, then let our feelings flow" *(mmmm, that's right, hotshot).*

"Good . . . See you on Thursday, Mr. Cheese 😊 I look forward to getting to know you—but will be less surprised than you (having seen more from you already than you from me 😌)"

"Typical woman 😉 But I have nothing to hide."

"Haha—maybe you should meet-up with a man?"

"Are you kidding?!"

"I am always kidding 😜 I hope there's more behind Jack than cheese 😊"

"Let me surprise you. I am a feelings person. And very creative . . . "

"I love surprises 😍"

"Also when having sex 👍"

"Nice 😊"

"I hope for a warm summer evening 💋"

"Feelings, creative and sex—you may be able to convince me with that . . ."

" . . . I don't like heart and hurt . . . Good mix . . . creative sex and feelings . . . some women wish for that, I think . . . but also men . . ."

"I am not ready for a 'love story', if that is what you mean . . . But a friend to laugh, have a good time, and wild sex with … I'm in for that."

"Definitely. Again and again. Spontaneous sex. It can only be good if two cheese nations come together."

"But still, you cannot influence feelings . . . hahaha let's meet, Mr Cheese 😘"

"No worries, I don't want a steady relation . . ."

"Worries are for tomorrow. And if today I am happy, tomorrow I will have no worries."

The stars look different today ...

-David Bowie

Wednesday, July 6th 2016
MORE FEELINGS

I can go on and on with the texting, as there's kilometres of it. Business, interests, funny stories, pictures. So much in so little time. He's asked me to check out his website, and I am impressed with the presentation of the group's fine products. He's handsome, and I tell him so.

How come I feel I know him? I like him a lot after all the writing, and I am looking forward to Thursday. The desire to meet has only grown stronger. This is no longer about 'feeling good'. I already feel good with myself. Thanks to two and a half months with Hot Date #1. This is about feelings—from my side, anyway. I cannot guess his side over the phone. Scary. But as I am a 'whole' person, I want to find out.

"When is it finally Thursday?," he wrote me yesterday. This remained on my mind all of today.

As I always do while on the road, I stopped at a parking area to text him. Being my impulsive self, I decided to call him instead, as I badly wanted to hear his voice. Voice is important to me. Calm, but at the same time not calm. Pleasant. Vibrant. Sexy. It's a bit awkward, as I don't know what to say. I was not prepared for this, and as you know, I cannot be spontaneous if I'm nervous. Aïe . . . the feeling got strong again. I have a knot in my belly. Intuition?

I meet up with Cuban Sex-god. He tells me my eyes look different again, and that I was not as forthcoming with my messages as I used to be. Am I pushing him away? (*Am I?*) I tell him he's not as forthcoming as he used to be either, to which he replies he doesn't want to disturb me, as he knows I am working on a lot of stuff at the moment. *Yeah, sure! You still believe once you have it, it's yours, right? Wrong, Señor. The same thing applies to you: If you want something, you have to work for it. It's that simple.* I tell him I like texting. Makes me feel good and wanted. And yes, I am pushing the thought of him away more, as I need to concentrate on my projects. I tell him I cancelled my operation.

Fuck, I don't know what I want anymore.

I make dinner, which is divine; and the sex, for the first time since we've met, is mediocre. Very.

*A man travels the world over
in search of what he needs
and returns home to find it*

-George A. Moore

Friday, July 8th 2016
WHAT DO MEN WANT?

I am so confused. The knot in my stomach has grown, and I am all emotional. I am not happy today, as I do not understand what happened last night.

Yesterday morning, I sent Jack a message to 'watch out . . . I am now a certified Matador'. I mean, since he is Taurus.

Last night, I was having a nice conversation with a Dutch couple I had just met at a street café, when Jack arrived, a bit late. Wow . . . Striking. Feeling a bit awkward, perhaps, but at the same time suggesting a predatory nature. He smiled. Mmmm, I liked it. Mucho.

We drink and talk about ourselves. I am appreciative about his having turned his passion into a business. So few people are actually daring to live their passion. I admire that. I explain how I've gone from boss to student, and ended up with who I am today. I talk about my projects. After a while, I tell him he's to show me the town, as I don't know it as of yet. I feel like leaving. I don't want other people around, or at least not that close. He suggests going to the lakeside, but worries that may be a bit of a challenge for me with my heels. I tell him not to worry, as shoes can be taken off. He's brought me cheese and yoghurts, which I will feast on for breakfast later on at home.

We sit down on the shore, drinks in hand, and talk some more. His father carries the same name as my grandad and my brother. His phone number contains both my year of birth and the number of the house in which I was born. I find out a bit more about him. But not enough. I sense he wants to talk, but somehow can't. We kiss. He tells me I am a beautiful woman. We feel and caress each other. He tells me he wants me. Too much. I *feel* too much. My intuition was right. And this scares the hell out of me.

He tells me I make him nervous. *Hell, I make him nervous? I'm scared shitless myself!* I tell him I won't bite. *But why am I making him nervous?* He doesn't explain. Jack's not a man of many words tonight. But I do believe he could be. Dominantly so. He asks if he says he wants to meet me another time, will I still come? I tell him I would. It's his first meet through this casual dating site, and this makes him anxious. I don't believe that is what makes him squirm, though. I believe I scare his feelings. *Were my honesty and the parts of my life story I was willing to tell him last night too much? Fuck, he doesn't know the half of it yet.* There's a whirlwind of emotions flying right through us, and neither wants to comment on it. I clearly feel I excite him, and he feels he excites me, but he backs out. I don't want him to. I have a need to find out more what my feelings are all about. And I'm not talking sex here. But I let him go anyway. I feel that it all has to come from his side this time. He asks me what I want. I say that I want him to take me home.

Now how much clearer can you be?

I didn't ask for sex. I may have provoked him a little, but only in reaction to his actions. I told him I felt good and safe in his strong arms while sitting and watching the sun go down, and I said that I wanted him to take me home with him. Not sex. Home. *This* is the moment he should have become nervous, not before. I would have been happy lying in his arms all night without making love. Should I have told him that?

We climb into the car, he takes me back to town, drops me off next to my car, and drives off. Bat out of hell.

What is this man scared of? Why does he try to escape feelings he will not be able to escape forever? Did he not understand the part where I told him I no longer care about materialistic matters and why? Did he not understand where I come from? Indeed, I was not ready for a serious relation, as I had told him upon meeting him. I still have so many doors to close. But I feel I am so about to slam them shut all at once. Hell, I feel so ready *now*. And this man . . . well . . . I definitely would want to give him *more* than a try.

Or has he been hurt so much that he doesn't want to face his feelings any longer? Well, muchacho, sooner or later you will have to . . . And let's face it. For the first time since starting this diary, the doubting and the questions are not on me!

I dreamt about Jack last night. Intense. But somehow, he disconcerts me.

Hot Date #1 texted me this afternoon, and I reply that I am writing, and that I could really do with some strong arms, as I'm so confused— without elaborating, of course. He tells me to be strong and enjoy the sun. I let him know I don't feel like being strong today. *Oh, fuck you, Hot Date! I know I'm like Superwoman to you, but deep down I'm only human. I cannot always be strong. And I would really want you to just hold me right now.*

I am no longer just emotional. The tears are really streaming down. *He, who gave me back so much of myself, cannot ever be a friend to me.*

You see, *my* Hot Date #1 will never be more than what it started out to be 2.5 months ago: a Hot Date. And he still is #1. I never got to #2 or #3. Not really. Because in my eyes they were not 'hot': they didn't acknowledge any of my needs, the emotions that craved for caressing. I will never find a 'true' Hot Date in this scene, not by lack of interest from the male casual community, but because however hard I try, I cannot do casual.

He, whom I talked with, shared my emotions with. He, whom I truly wanted to be my 'friend with benefits'. He, who knows so much about me, and still doesn't 'get' me. Or doesn't care . . . For a real friend would have asked 'what's wrong' or would've come over to me straightaway, and would have taken me in his arms without asking any questions.

And this realization makes me scream out with frustration. Because I am no longer content with what I had for the last two and a half months. And although I will be eternally grateful for what he has done — without him understanding even a fraction of what exactly it is that he's given me (even though he's read the first part of my diary) —, I realize that I must have known deep down from the beginning that at some point I would have to let him go. *Hot sex, him appreciating me, and me being grateful for the feelings he gave me is no longer enough.* There where I was safe rediscovering my femininity and sexuality, there where I made my feelings whole again, there where I was reborn into an even stronger woman than I used to be before my marriage collapsed. That place is no longer mine to occupy. I now have to start again on my own strength. This cannot continue for much longer. And he probably will not understand why the day I tell him I can no longer see him. Our drums beat out of tune. His, still casual, I believe; mine, on a heartbeat. I only wish he would have allowed me to know him the way he now knows me. Feelings included. I am scared of being all alone.

But before letting him go, I will need him to explain what a man wants from a woman. Even though his wanting may be a bit 'off' from the general male opinion, I may be able to figure it all out.

On a different note, this Jack thing is getting to me as well.

Bi the way,
coming out
was never easy

Saturday, July 9th 2016
WTF, JACK

I sent Jack 2 pictures yesterday, a 'life is good' one with my dog coming out of the water, and a 'breakfast was wonderful' with an empty yoghurt pot. No reply. Did he feel awkward? I believe I would have. But he shouldn't. I understand. I was not feeling too great myself yesterday.

Late evening:

> "Sleep well 😙"
>
> "I dreamt about you last night . . . Noooo . . . Dreams immensely private . . . You ok?"

I dreamt about him again last night. And decide that that's it. If I have to have patience, that's OK. But I am not going to be ignored.

> "If I told you about my feelings, would you be less anxious? Or do I need to leave you alone for a while?"
>
> "You should not leave me alone 👄"
>
> "Ok—then talk to me. Go for a walk tonight?"
>
> ". . . going for beers with a friend . . ."
>
> "Good 😊 Have fun!"

He's still scared and doesn't want to know about my feelings, or at least fails to confirm he wants to know. But he did write that I shouldn't leave him alone . . . complete with kissing lips. His turn now. I'm lost.

Back to Hot Date #1 . . .

> "Hola, hombre—you ok? Had a nice w/end with the girls? 😙"

"Hola, Bella. Yes, very nice. Girls have gone home. I will have a shower to cool down" *(mmm really . . . he's doing it on purpose, putting pictures in my mind)*. "And you, how are you? 😊 😗"

"Exhausted—was alone all w/end, kids gone to music festival—been running and got a lot of writing and research done. Outside. Now all hyped-up 😊 Just had pizza with kids 😊 Ate too much 😵 😵 Still no reply to my question from last week? Not a problem, but I would like to have your input in any case to have a full circle. Now have a pretty good idea after a w/end research 😊 Sueños salvajes, señor 😼"

"Ciao, yes, I will give you an answer when we see each other. Not per messaging. Sleep well, gracias 😗"

" 😗 "

" 😊 😗 "

And then, Jack sends me some beautiful views from the mountains and lets me know he'd gone for a long walk and cooled down in a well. With no swimming trunks. *Really, Jack. Teasing but no talking?*

Any product that needs a manual to work is broken ….

-Elon Musk

Monday, July 11th 2016
ONE OF A KIND

When finishing off my e-mails this afternoon, my mind wandered to Jack and Hot Date #1. How I wished I was only a tiny bit more like Hot Date #1 . . . You like, you do. No complications.

And then, all of a sudden, it hit me . . . Jack likes, but maybe Jack cannot 'just do'? Much like me. Is it possible that there are men out there in that parallel world that have to have feelings to do the deed? Or, when feeling too much and being unsure about their partners' intentions, will back out?

This brings a smile on my face, and I text Jack right away. *Cheese finished, yoghurt finished, now what?* He's read the message, but no reply . . . Do I have to keep provoking him? He said he didn't want me to leave him alone for a while. Maybe I should do exactly that anyway. Why do I always have to run into men who should come with instruction manuals?

Fuck them all—I'm going for a run!

Stood up,
curtsied,
and moved on.

Tuesday, July 12th 2016
STOOD UP AGAIN?

Hot Date #1 is extremely tired. So tired that neither while or after work did he reply to my WhatsApp. Nor to my texting late afternoon. And yes, he finally says he's sorry, he'd fallen asleep, and he's soooo tired that we should see each other the following week. Have you ever had a fight by text/WhatsApp messages? Here's how that goes:

"Glad you're ok"

"I'm very tired 😌"

"You fuck around too much, muchacho . . ."

"Sorry"

"Nah, you're not . . . I'm really pissed off, hombre. Believe I've been open & honest w/ you so far. Not asking for anything but you being straight w/ me. And believe this time is one too many. I'm really disappointed."

"Sorry, I cannot force myself. I'm telling you the truth 🌷" (at least he got that I didn't like roses, right?)

"If you want it, work for it. It's that simple."

"Yes, but not today."

"Oh, man . . . forget about it. I like you a lot and I love to make love to you, but I hate being fucked around. And that's how I feel right now. I do get it that you're tired. You're getting old, señor. What you don't get is that I don't care. I'd be happy to just have a coffee or a drink w/ you (prefer sex, of course, not gonna lie), or lie down w/ you to give you a massage, cause that's who and how I am. Let me know whether I should be looking for a Hot Date #2."

"I had a hard day today. I just want, I need, to go to bed early. If you have that need to find someone else, that's ok. It's your

255

life. Sorry. Hope you understand."

"Oh, fuck it, you know me well enough to know I have no need for multiple men in my life. I'm only disappointed as first you don't bother replying to messages, then have me worried, and then cancel on me. Call me when you are not tired."

"Gracias for your understanding" *(I don't understand anything, asshole, why not explain?)*

Of course, as usual, neither Hot Date #2 nor Hot Date #3 are available when you need them most. Guess some things are just meant not to happen.

Analysing options does not always mean calculating.
Many times, it is just getting rid of one equation or another ...

Wednesday, July 13th 2016
SAY SORRY. YAIKS!

"Hola, hombre, it would make me so happy if we could meet this week . . . No sex—it's your turn to talk and my turn to listen. I have spoken enough. I am a true Capricorn, but must have some vicious Scorpio influence, as I am a hothead and sometimes extremely bitchy 😊" *(have to fucking apologize to get what I'm after . . .)*

"Ciao, Bella, I just got home from work and will go to Basel tonight. I will be in Italy until Saturday, and back home on Sunday evening. I hope you are well 😘"

"I'm not 'Superwoman', so no, not really . . . No worries, I'm a survivor 🙂 Have fun 😘"

"Gracias, and have a good week, hasta pronto 😘"

Yeah, right . . .

Nature doesn't give a damn for convenience,
and never has …

-Lara Adrian

Friday, July 15th 2016
SOUL SISTER

I picked up my soul sister early to have a coffee before training. Needed to talk about all this. About being conflicted. What is it with this Cuban that makes me want to find out about his motivation? Why can I not let things be? Why can I not enjoy his company when he's there and forget about him when he's not? Why do I have this 'need' for him to be the friend that he'll never be?

She tells me it's just part of me. I am certainly no easy quitter. I should not question myself about what makes him stay around this long. As far as she's concerned, to him it's the convenience of having someone around for good sex. Anything else, he's not interested in. Either forget about him and cut off all ties, or enjoy whenever he's there.

I tell her I cannot do this anymore. Perhaps with someone else. But not with him. Not after what he's given me. And I'm ready to cry again (but won't let myself). She tells me maybe it is time to move on to the next level: check out more serious sites to find a 'real' partner instead of a casual one. You know what? She may be right.

*The only queer people
are those who do not love anybody.*

-*Rita Mae Brown*

Saturday, July 16th 2016
TWIN SISTER

Tonight, I drive 1.5 hours to a 'Dutch' gathering. Lots of fun, and I get to know some new expats in this country. Of course, my twin sister is there as well, and I tell her all about my new find, Jack, and that I am puzzled. She takes a look at his picture and risks the possibility of a gay past. According to her, the man is probably as much aroused as confused. Interesting hypothesis. I decide to leave him be. I couldn't care less anymore. I have no more time for this. I'm tired of playing games. Not with Jack and not with Hot Date #1. I want a friend. Male. But have to see Cuban lover boy one more time to have *his* side of *my* story.

The penis mightier than the sword ...

-Unknown

Friday, July 22nd 2016
EINSTEIN

I don't get to see Hot Date #1 this week either. That will make 3 weeks of no Hot Date on our next meet. It's a record. Instead, I attend a concert with my kids.

In his texting, Cuban lover boy betrays his astonishment when asking for confirmation, as he makes it clear he will not be available for the rest of the week. *I don't care anymore, Hot Date #1! Do you truly believe that I would cancel a concert with my kids to meet up with you? You must be kidding! Need to get your priorities straight, señor.* Some doubting cannot do any harm . . .

What a wonderful evening it is: my kids, good food, and fine music. And that is all I need that night: seeing my kids happy.

Hot Date #1 writes me the next day to know how the concert had been (he calls me beautiful). I tell him it was cool, fun, and with lots of laughter. I tell him that today I had lunch with my 'unruly four', together with laughs, sun, and a dip into the lake. They are crazy. "Like you," he says. With a smiley.

Right. It is hot and I am hot, so I tell him, *'j'ai envie de toi'* (I want you). Google Translate comes up with a poor translation, which he does not understand. The meaning of 'envie' is stronger than wanting, but not quite as strong as craving; perhaps desiring, depending on the context. I do not wait for a reaction: 'Guess what I am thinking of doing to you right now.' That makes him laugh. Instead of waiting till next Tuesday, he may be available Sunday evening . . . I reply that I may not be able to wait that long *(in Spanish . . . point to self)*. Maybe I will, maybe I won't.

I checked back on the site yesterday, first time in 2 weeks, as I was curious and also felt a bit lonely. Home alone. And since Hot Date #1 didn't have time for me this week, I thought I could try 'no feelings'. The inhumanly beautiful 22-year-old is on to me again. But how am I going to live with myself if I accept to go out with a 22-year-old, right? As before, it was not meant to happen . . . I am still curious as to the whys of a 22-year-old hottie.

While online, I receive a message from Einstein saying that I was suggested to him, as we seem to share interests. He also asks about the type of man I am interested in. This is how this one starts off:

> "Not looking for a 'type' of man. I like to be charmed, I like to be seduced, I like to go out and laugh a lot, and I like long hot nights if the person pleases me 😊 I am looking for one-night stands 😳 Oh, that went wrong . . . I am NOT interested in one-night stands . . ."

> "Funny. Missing NOT is common on this site. What is your origin? I am German. And you?"

> "I'm Dutch . . . And a 'NOT' makes such a difference 😌"

> "👍😎"

> "What do you do in town?"

> "I am in the tobacco business. Living here since 2007. Earlier on the other side of the country. Ever tried snorting tequila?"

> "I used to be in corporate business; recently completed further studies. Snorting tequila? Explain . . . 😵"

> "Can't do in writing. Need to try . . ."

> "Nice . . . classy . . . There's a bar in town called Einstein. They have a cigar room."

> "You smoke cigars?"

> "Mmmmm . . . must try everything at least once in your life, right?"

"Deal! Name? Photo?"

"Cigarillos sometimes . . . not a huge fan . . . but am great in determining whether a cigar is good with my nose" (keep coming back to the snorting, right?)

"Send me your e-mail or mobile—will send pronto"

"Your nose will not be the same."

"After the tequila snorting or after your cigars? hahaha"

"Need to warn you. Snorting is a once only. Only the tough ones do more than once"

"One-night snorting . . . hahaha 😵 But am serious, though . . . If you are looking for a one-nighter, better look further. I am not after a 'permanent' deal in the near future (recently started separation procedure)—but am soooo tired of being my best self ALL the time . . . I want a friend with benefits."

Some time later,

"Still stalking me?"

"oh, fuck .. got me there . . . (that was hours ago, btw). Didn't you need to go shopping? Not stalking, snorting . . . started w/out you 😊 Trying to rid myself of all these weirdos, but they keep coming back 😠"

"Bbq is on fire. Do not drop all your picks too early. You do not know how weird I am. The 22 y/o who approached me earlier today is still on my search list 👍 Will be fun when I ask my 21 y/o daughter to call her mom"

"Hahaha. Well, I'm Dutch and in your eyes automatically weird. Soooo . . . Btw, the 22-year-old should be on your bucket list. 😬 And don't worry, you do not have to search for her—she'll find you 😺 Was the BBQ ok, even though spare ribs & steaks burned?"

"On my way to a golf match over the w/end. Back Monday

night. Should give you enough time to figure out how to best impress me 😎"

"Oh, but I do know, Einstein . . . My sheer presence will blind you 😇 What about you? Figured out how to impress me? Btw, I dreamt about you last night . . ."

And then, I log off. In between, there's been a lot of WhatsApping. Ahhh, he's extremely funny. He makes me laugh (a lot), and he's cute (for a 52-year-old). I decide that he could be my friend. Wait and see . . .

$E=MC2...$
I have a different theory.

Saturday, July 23rd 2016
MORE EINSTEIN THAN IS GOOD FOR ME

"You are already mine. You may ignore that for now, but you will be lost from the moment of first 'live' contact—YOU know that we are riding the same wave" *(Aaaahhhh, a macho man, I knew it . . . controlling . . . I want more . . . I am already lost . . . come and find me . . . please . . .)*

"Aïe, that's putting pictures in my mind, señor. Not fair. Words come easy, Einstein, and pleasing they are, I admit 😊 But now you have to live up to them, and that may be more difficult because of the mentioned pictures. Do I need sunglasses, Einstein? 😳"

Ohlala, Einstein is getting to me. As he's German and away for the weekend, perhaps I'll wear my Bavarian dress on our first meet to make him laugh . . . Or find a Matador outfit . . . Aïe. Einstein definitely an interesting prospect!

Strong character is brought out by change,
weak ones by permanence.

-Jean Paul

Sunday, July 24th 2016
I SOMEHOW KNEW

"Enjoy the 'head' movie" (*took me some time to figure out, but he meant the pictures he put in my head*). "No glasses needed. As long as you do not undress after 1 min, we are ok. After 5 min it is acceptable."

"Ok, no sunglasses. Ok, no undressing after 1 min (whatever were you thinking Einstein, I'm a decent girl). Enjoy your w/end 😘"

"Sure, you are decent. No doubt. To be confirmed next week. Have a nice w/end."

😇

I met up with Hot Date #1 last night, and somehow it's becoming cozy. Sex still good and enjoyable, but less intense. Too much hassle and power struggles, I guess.

As to my question about what it would take to 'have' a woman like me, he replied, "Who wouldn't want to be with you?" I found that a bit easy and not very well thought-through . . . So I inquire further. Apparently, as I am a really strong-willed woman who knows what she wants (*hmmm*), I would need either a man who can adapt himself easily (*i.e. I would wipe the floor with him?*), or someone who also has a strong character (*more power struggles?*) with whom I could either work together or share similar interests. Thank you, Hot Date #1, that was exactly what I had in mind (the latter, I mean). But honestly, it took you three weeks to come up with this?

Smoking cigars is like falling for someone.
First, you're attracted by its shape;
you stay for its flavor,
and you must always remember never,
never to let the flame go out.

-Sir Winston Churchill

Monday, July 25th 2016
MORE EINSTEIN

> "Sure, you are innocent. You missed the part where you tell me that you are still a virgin, right? Any idea when and where we shall date?"

> "Haha, didn't pretend to be. But with the number of penile screenshots I got forced in my face, thought I'd warn you 😇 Thursday would be convenient for me. You ok with that?"

> "Ok 4 me"

> "Well, Einstein, why don't you propose where you can make a girl laugh? 😊"

He sends me a picture with an extremely sexy lady smoking a cigar, with the text: 'Given the choice between a woman and a cigar . . . always choose the woman with a cigar'. Mentioning that the picture shows the recommended dress code.

> "That would be 'Undressed' style from Marlies Dekkers . . . I never ever wear that on a first date . . . You'd fall off your chair 😌"

> "Isn't that what you want? Knock me off my chair when I see you?"

> "Maybe . . ."

> "Funny you mention 'not on a first date' . . . How about jumping immediately to date 2?"

> "Noooo . . . I want to be seduced on a first date . . ."

> "What do you want to tell me here?"

> "I'm a witch 😇"

> "Yeah, that's what I figured out already . . . Innocent witch . . ."

"Siii . . . But very straight and honest . . ."

"Goooood, love that"

"Like you too, Einstein 😇"

"Wait and see. But you are lost, anyway . . ."

"Mmmm. I do not care about looks, Einstein, I do care about personality . . ."

"But if you have both you won't complain"

"Now, Einstein . . . What are you looking for?"

"Personal trainer"

"Haha, need to work on your endurance? I'm a marathoner . . ."

"Aaaah, had something else in mind"

"That too . . ."

"😂😂😂😂😂"

"Got to go, Einstein, duty's calling 😘"

*Sometimes, a man's purpose in a woman's life
is to help her become a better woman ...*

For another man.

Wednesday, August 3rd 2016
THE ARTIST

A lot has gone on in the last week and a half. Only one meet with Hot Date #1, who all of a sudden is not that hot to me anymore. Still nice. Sex still good, but my mind is no longer in it. I want more. I need to close those last doors so I am truly free to explore further.

Einstein cancels our date. Family issues. I sympathize. Family is family, and if there's trouble you have to take care of it. I am not in a rush with Einstein. I really like him and would like him to be the *he* I so long for. Wishful thinking? Projecting inner feelings?

I work hard on my projects, as the job I applied for fell through: internal promotion. Will need to find investors now, and continue chasing the owner of the house I 'have to have' again.

I don't ask Hot Date #1 whether we were on for last night. Had he wanted to see me, he would've asked. I told him more than enough that he should be straight and ask/say what he wants. If he still doesn't get it . . . So instead, I went to see the Artist. I agreed to meet with the painter whom I, having seen his work, would have liked to make the cover of my book. Alas . . . the cover of my book now needs another artist.

He is practically aggressive in his approach by text. But not so in real life. He talks a load of bull. How meeting different women has changed his approach, how he had been timid before and now knows all about women. *Yeah, right!* I am not that interested anymore, but rather frustrated with his attitude. If I want to be painted, I need to feel some spiritual connection with the artist. I look at his paintings again, and he reaches out and starts caressing my back gently. His hands are too soft, not enough power in them to lift my spirits. But when he moves in to me, I feel that I excite him and that in turn excites me. I am not attracted to him. Not to his body, nor to his mind. How does he still manage to excite me? That makes me curious, and I am disgusted with myself for wanting to find out.

We start kissing (*not a very good kisser; that should have warned me!*) and we end up on the couch. I do like the way he treats my nipples, though, so being my stupid self, I want to see where this ends up. Right. It ends up between my breasts. Party over. Lesson learned. If not attracted, there's a reason for it . . .

Laughter has no foreign accent.

-Paul Lowney

Monday, August 8th 2016
SUN, BEACH AND BUM(MER)S

Always expect the unexpected. Einstein's back. . .

"Hi, Tequila, how was your long w/end back home? Need someone to apply your after-sun lotion?"

"Hi, Einstein, still away, drive back on Tuesday. Was on the beach on Saturday, cloudy & windy, so no need for after-sun care—but I could pretend if you insist 😇"

"Too bad you're not back yet, could have offered only tonight or tomorrow for a personal training session. Thanks for your flexibility to pretend if needed . . . Makes life so much easier. Take care."

"Late night? Bad night?"

"Bad"

"Oh, Einstein . . . I thought YOU were the one in need of personal training . . ."

"Yes, I am"

"Bad nights are not good . . . Don't know why . . ."

"No, prefer practice nights . . ."

". . . But somehow wanna make you feel better"

"Thanks"

"Noooo . . . thanks comes when you DO feel better . . ."

"Which treat are you thinking of?"

I send him a picture of the hotel I was staying at last Saturday.

"This would have been soooo nice for a first meet . . . Was thinking of laugh therapy . . . The best therapy to make you feel good . . ."

"Goooood"

We talk some more about my home country and the coast, and I ask him if he's ever been there. He tells me he learned surfing on the lakes in the North some 30 years ago, to which I reply I was on a sailing holiday on those lakes and around the isles. He mentions that we are about the same age, on which I observe that only approximately— unless he lied about his age on the site.

"Am 64."

"Oooooh, so laugh therapy actually is the only way to make you feel good." 😇

"Born in 64, not dead."

"I do hope not . . . And I know what you meant . . . I am an incorrigible kidder."

"Me too."

"I know. I am very attracted to your writing, Mr. Einstein. Better meet soon so as not to be disappointed."

"You are not in town."

"Ahhh nooo; plus you are too busy. Will we ever meet?"

"Soooorry . . . If there is a God for funny dates, we shall meet. What time are you back Tuesday?"

"No, don't be sorry. Sorry comes only after a bad night. I'll be back late" *(and even if I were early, I wouldn't schedule a date after having driven for 800 km non-stop, my dear Einstein).*

"Too bad."

"I have patience . . . but not a lot."

"Me neither."

"I know . . . Next avail date?"

"Tuesday 16th."

"Ok for me. Got to run, Einstein. Have a meeting at 09h00 and am still in my (now cold) bath . . . Enjoy your week 😖"

"Deal."

Nobody dies from lack of sex.
It's lack of love we die from ...

-*Margaret Atwood*

Thursday, August 11th 2016
NOW WHAT?

I met for drinks and a nice evening out with Hot Date #1 yesterday, and realize again that this has to stop. Hot Date #1 is still hot, mind you, but my thoughts are elsewhere.

During a break, I tell him I have a problem and would like him to give me an answer. I ask him what to do if one day I am in love and the sex is not as fulfilling as it is with him. "Are you in love?", he asks me. Well, of course not . . . otherwise I would not be here, right? I truly *am* conflicted over this, as my feelings would not allow me to be in love with one man and have sex with another. He tells me that basically you should be able to separate the two, if that were the case. I tell him I can't. End of conversation.

Can't say I have ever been too fond of beginnings myself.
Messy little things.
Give me a good ending anytime.
You know where you are with an ending.

-*Neil Gaiman*

Sunday, August 14th 2016
CONFUSION RULES

> "Hi, Tequila, am terribly sorry, but this casual dating is killing my life. Need a break. Too much mental confusion. Need to sort out my life first. Forgive me, but right now is not a good time to date me. Wish you all the best, and maybe one day we can catch up again. Sorry, not your fault, it's me. Be good. Einstein."

And there you have it. After Hot Date #1 to make me feel good, Jack 'the runner' to project my feelings on, and The Artist to see how selfish selfish can be, I feel deeply sad. But happy at the same time.

> "I know. We are on the same level, you and me, Einstein. I knew in the back of my mind that you were going to cancel again. I only wanted to meet to 'feel' whether my instinct was right about you, and was not going to sleep with you anyway (maybe to come back one day when ready) . . . So, in a way, it doesn't change. Except that now I cannot confirm my instinct. But I've lived with worse. I'll get over it 😉

> In April, I needed this casual dating to move myself back on track, and managed to do just that through one casual affair that lasted close to 5 months. Which is why I mentioned to you in our first conversation that I didn't want a one-night stand. I wanted a friend. At the same time, as you, I still have some doors to close before moving on to the next level.

> Although we never spoke or met, I could read between the lines and felt that there was more to Einstein.

> Life happens today, yesterday cannot be repeated, and tomorrow may never come.

> Try to be happy, Einstein. Always. Whatever shit is coming your way. There are no problems, only solutions. We may

285

meet one day. And if not, it wasn't meant to be. If you need an anonymous friend to spill your guts with, you know where to find me."

"Thanks for your inspiring and understanding words. One first has to be free to open new chapters in life. At least I found a good soul, even though we never met. Future will tell what good may come out of it. Take good care."

"And you, Einstein . . . Stay strong, that's how I 'see' you 😊"

"Usually am. But even strong men sometimes need a sounding board . . ."

"I know—that's why I told you to contact me when in need to spill your guts . . ."

"Your number stays in my contacts."

"I like that 😊"

I love the sound of my feet
walking away from things not meant for me ...

-Unknown

Tuesday, August 23rd 2016

I TRIED, YOU DIDN'T. I'M DONE. HAVE FUN!

> "Ciao, Bella. Sorry for not replying sooner. I want to try and concentrate on my relation *(after 7 years? Yeah, right!)* and that's why I want to back out of adventures right now. Sorry, it was really good with you. But you cannot have it all *(and why not, Hot Date? I believe I can).* Maybe it is just a phase that, who knows, lasts one day or maybe forever *(trying to keep the door open? Oh, forget it, my lover-boy!)* I don't know. Wish you a nice day. Kiss 😊"

Hot Date #1 has had enough. Not sure whether I am too much or whether he needs a change, but I don't care anymore. Mentally, I was already finished with him a long time ago. Done with the analyzing. Done with the casual scene. I am not casual, so why did I try to be someone I am not?

> "Shite, grow up, be a man and say what you want for once . . . I am not a retard and have known for some time . . . But by text? Really? After all I shared with you? Fuck, mate, that hurts!"

> "We can talk if you like"

> "Nah . . . It's ok—I have talked enough and you don't speak about your feelings . . . but I do not understand how, after 4 months, you 'break up' via texting . . . I knew you weren't long-term material, and I was not looking for it. But by text? Not so classy from your side . . . I am disappointed. All a woman wants is a man to be honest with her and speak his mind . . . No worries, I have lived worse."

So . . . Hot Date # 1 is finally out of the picture. For good. No regrets.

I will miss the sex, though . . .

Knowing yourself is the beginning of all wisdom.

-Aristotle

Wednesday, August 24th 2016
UNDECIDED

Last night, I went and did one of these online intelligence tests, and yes, Einstein (the real one, Albert) came up. As he does on a regular basis lately. I decided to send a screenshot of the test to Einstein.

"It keeps coming back all the time, Einstein . . ."

"Sorry 4 being a genius . . ." *(see what I mean? Only he can reply like this and still make me laugh.)*

"😊"

"You ok?"

"Undecided."

"You don't strike me as an undecided person . . . Go for what you 'feel' is good for you, Einstein, the rest will fall in place."

"Too many confusing impressions."

"Oh . . . Casuals?"

"Women in general."

"Haha. You're a big boy. You figure it out 😁 You have an education. Dissect what you do not understand; and ignore what you'll never understand."

"👍😎"

"CU soon, Einstein 😚 Gotta run—literally."

"Take care and stay in shape. Competition is tough."

"There is no such thing as competition if you know what you're worth . . . 😚"

Well, Einstein, this should give you something to think about if you are able to comprehend. And I think you will.

The whole world thinks in terms of competition. I have come to understand it all differently. In business terms, you may *try* to compete. But if you know what you are worth and you present yourself in that manner, it's the relation you have built over time with your business partner what determines whether the deal is made or not. I believe I have always known this on a subconscious level.

Life follows a course of its own. You can influence it by being open to constant learning on different subjects, and, more importantly, about yourself. Stay open. Stay focused. Even when things will always happen the way they should. And you can either go with the flow and let it take you down, *or* you can learn from it and be creative about finding solutions to swim up to your next level.

And now I finally know.

I am allowed to have weaknesses; I am allowed to dream and live my dreams, make them come true; I always try to make fun of unpleasant and even hard situations . . . that's just what I do. And I feel soooo much, sometimes too much. And that is OK as well.

And now I want it all. And I will have it all. I will not search, because I know it will come to me when it is time . . .

I have completed this painting
I gathered my memories and learnings, my utensils,
to create a new masterpiece ...

Even a rock moves on.

EPILOGUE

"Life is short, break the rules, forgive quickly, kiss slowly, love truly, laugh uncontrollably, and never regret anything that made you smile. Twenty years from now, you will be more disappointed by the things you didn't do than by the ones you did. So throw off the bowlines. Sail—away from the safe harbour. Catch the trade winds in your sails. Explore. Dream. Discover."

—Mark Twain

And I did . . .

I did realize that life is short *(and something needed to be done immediately)*.

I did break all the rules *(and I still do . . . even the unwritten ones)*.

I do forgive quickly *(for that is my kind spirit)*.

I do kiss slowly *(and passionately . . . and really a lot when given the opportunity)*.

I do love truly *(with heart, soul, and body)*.

I do laugh uncontrollably on many occasions, and I will never ever regret anything that made me smile.

Twenty years from now, I will not be disappointed. Because I literally took the bull by the horns and did everything that God forbade *(and I'm still not finished. So many challenges still out there . . .)*

I threw off the bowlines and sailed away from my safe *(and painful)* harbor.

I didn't catch the trade winds in my sails, though. It was a *fucking* hurricane!

I explore *(deeply)*, I dream *(and will accomplish the best of my dreams)*, and I discovered *(though still have lots to learn)*.

I am Cassie. I am Tequila. Up until recently I was the woman a lot of you are today. But whatever my name is . . . I am real!

Now is your turn. And please, don't forget to write me about it on Facebook.

(https://www.facebook.com/thelifeofcassiedate)

You are fucking awesome!

Cassie Date

Cassie Date earned her degree in interior architecture at age 48. Marathoner, an optimist par excellence (sunny side up, always!). Ex-corporate bitch, CEO level. Business and art project developer. Bad mom (although her kids tend to disagree). Dreams of settling on the beach and writing full-time. With an inquisitive mind and a passion for life, art, and all that is beautiful. An architect of 'wonderings' and writing about it. Go find her on Facebook, Twitter, or YouTube. And write to her, yes . . . do write to her!

Be careful with this author . . . she writes about those things that you wouldn't dare.

The Fresh Ink Group

Publishing
Free Memberships
Free-Story Newsletter
Writing Contests

❧

Books
Ebooks

❧

Authors
Editors
Artists
Professionals
Publishing Services
Publisher Resources

❧

Members' Websites
Members' Blogs
Social Media

FreshInkGroup.com

Email: info@FreshInkGroup.com

Twitter: @FreshInkGroup

Google+: Fresh Ink Group

Facebook.com/FreshInkGroup

LinkedIn: Fresh Ink Group

Fresh Ink Group

Courageous Lady
The Lady Trilogy, Novel #1
Mark Allen North

Intrepid Lady
The Lady Trilogy, Novel #2
Mark Allen North

Valiant Lady
The Lady Trilogy, Novel #3
Mark Allen North

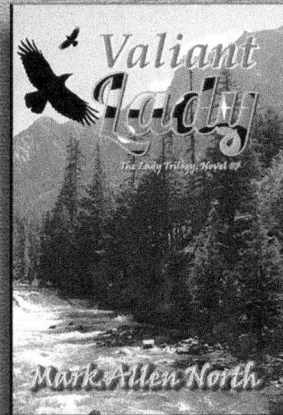

Leigh West travels to Alaska's majestic and mysterious Tongass National Forest in search of self-discovery and harmony with nature. In her journal, she chronicles all she learns from the cunning wolves, belligerent brown bears, and native Tlingit tribesmen. She marries one, adopts two, fights fire with vigor, and promotes environmental concerns all in the transforming seasons of the region's glorious landscape. It is through Native American spirituality that she sparks new passion within herself, a new appreciation for the physical world, and a life filled with love.

www.ingramcontent.com/pod-product-compliance
Lightning Source LLC
LaVergne TN
LVHW051456080426
835509LV00017B/1777